START QUICK

LEARN FAST

BE INSPIRED

PLAY BASS

PRAISE FOR *BASICS FOR BASSISTS*

"This is an epic book. I've never seen a more complete book for bassists."

Joe Escalante, The Vandals

"It's a rollicking good read."

Paul Gray, The Damned, Eddie & The Hot Rods, UFO

"*Basics for Bassists* is a delightful, clever, and intelligent read about the sleeper instrument: the bass guitar. With a good dose of humility and humor Murphy takes us on a colorful musical journey that earned him a 23-year career with the multi-platinum-awarded band Sugar Ray. Readable, comprehensible, and enjoyable – he makes it fun to learn. whether it's for writing songs, performing on stage, or teaching, his love of music will rub off on any budding bass guitarist."

Frank Simes, musical director, The Who, Roger Daltrey, Don Henley, Don Felder

"Informative and fun. I literally laughed out loud. Murphy breaks it down to the absolute basics. Not only for [learning] the bass, but for other important subjects like; "Understanding Your Role" or "Meeting People". I highly recommend this book."

Kevin Baldes, Lit

"SO much more than your standard instructional music book... I've never seen one of these books go so deep."

Bob Thomson, Big Drill Car

"As a self-taught musician, I wish I had this book as a primer when I snuck into my big sister's bedroom to practice on her guitar. With just the right amount of theory, professional tips, inspirational influences, and band history, this book isn't just perfect for beginners, but for early songwriters and career minded musicians as well."
Burke Thomas, Duff McKagan's Loaded, Vendetta Red, Roger Fisher

"I'm convinced that this is the best and quickest way to learning your instrument and understanding music. This book is not only for players, there's a lot here for instructors as well!"
Andy Stoller, Tracy Chapman, Ann Wilson

"Rife with anecdotes and musings, *Basics for Bassists* will put you ahead of the game and immune to a lot of bad decision making."
Kellii Scott, Failure

"A must-read for anyone thinking about picking up a bass."
Greg Camp, Grammy Award-nominated songwriter, The Defiant, formerly of Smash Mouth

"My bass brother Murphy Karges has put together an enjoyable and comprehensive book for beginners – a great place to start!"
Mike Inez

"This book really delivers! Real world applications from an experienced Rock Star with everything you would need to become a gigging musician."
Marty Schwartz, Marty Music

"Murph gives you the nuts and bolts of bass design all the way
to having tunes on heavy radio rotation and playing for huge
crowds. If you are just bass curious or have been playing for
a few years there are many insights here to help you reach
the next level and discover your own voice and mission."
Steve Fossen, Heart, (Rock 'n Roll Hall of Fame Member)

"Wow! Murphy has written an outstanding book. there's an awful
lot of good information in here. I got to see him up close playing
some massive gigs and I can attest that he knows a thing or two,
'cos he's seen a thing or two."
Arion Salazar, Third Eye Blind

"I wish I had a book like this when I was a kid! Murphy takes you
on a fun and personal journey through the BASS-ics that anyone
with a desire to learn the bass would be smart to start with."
Justin Bivona, The Interrupters

"Murphy's experience as a performer and now educator shines
through every page, offering invaluable insights and techniques
for both novice and seasoned bassists alike. *Basics For Bassists*
goes beyond just technical instruction by diving into the artistry
and mindset essential to becoming a proficient all-around
bassist, ready to hit the stage!"
Jason Freese, Green Day, Joe Walsh, Goo Goo Dolls

"Informative, Simple, and FUN. Whether you're a beginner or a
professional there's something to learn from this book. I sure have."
Tim Hutton, Three Dog Night

BASICS FOR BASSISTS

OR HOW TO NOT SUCK AT PLAYING BASS!

MURPHY KARGES

OCEAN PRESS 36

ISBN: 979-8-9906934-0-1

Printed in the United States of America

Published by Ocean 36 Press

Design & Illustration: Paul Palmer-Edwards
Edited by Matt Price & Erica Karlin

For Stacy

CONTENTS

PHASE THREE: PUTTING IT TOGETHER

PHASE FOUR: NEXT STEPS

LEARN YOUR BASS-ICS

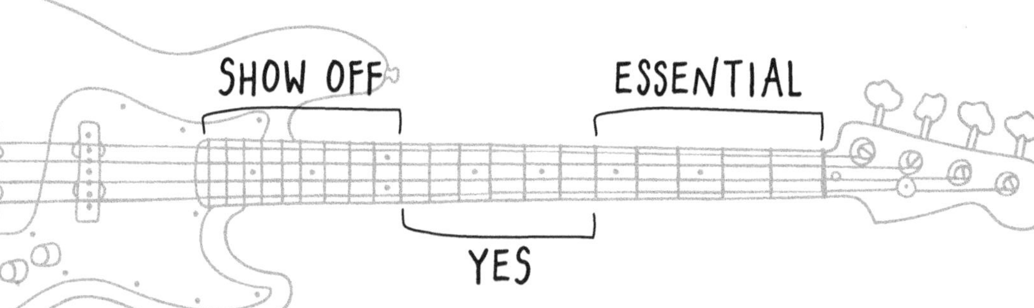

YOU *DON'T NEED TABS!* LEARN TO PLAY, *THEN* LEARN TO WRITE (MAYBE) AND SOMEDAY YOU WILL SHRED ON YOUR BASS BUT FIRST LET'S GO BACK TO THE BEGINNING...

INTRO

My band and I were standing inside Giants Stadium, waiting to play our six songs before Bon Jovi took the stage on a cool Friday night in the fall of 2001.

We were fresh off our hits "Every Morning" and "Someday," and we were in New York to do two nights in a row. The crowd was big, the biggest we'd ever played. Standing on a stage in front of 55,000 people might make you nervous, especially when you're holding your bass guitar waiting to play in front of a sea of people so vast and tightly arranged that it almost looks fake. But I wasn't having any panic attacks because I had been practicing my whole life for that moment. All the hours I spent in my room as a kid, practicing, playing bass and dreaming of going on tour in front of screaming fans were worth it.

And now it was happening.

Truth be told, some of the screams and echoes from the crowd were partially for us to get on with it so they could see their headliner: the kings of New Jersey, the champions of Johnny who still works on the dock. But it was mind-blowing just the same.

The dream had come true.

HOW IT ALL STARTED

My love for music goes back to when I was seven years old, sitting in the living room of my home in San Carlos, California, transfixed by the music coming from a record player in an old wood cabinet. I was drawn to that room because of the music, but also because my mom would sing along as she did chores around the house. Even though she was vacuuming or ironing or whatever, she seemed so happy listening to that music, and I wanted to find out what made her so happy.

I spent my afternoons in that room. I would lie on an oval rug in the middle of the floor, sunlight flooding in from a large window. My little fingers would scratch the needle of the record player to the beginning of records, letting them play, soaking in their sounds, listening to entire albums. My parents had a fantastic collection: The Rolling Stones, The Who, Elton John, Led Zeppelin, The Beatles, Cream, James Taylor, Joni Mitchell, Crosby, Stills & Nash, Seals & Crofts, Linda Ronstadt, Stevie Wonder, The Allman Brothers, Carole King, and dozens more.

But it was John, Paul, George & Ringo who most caught my attention. The Beatles seemed like they were doing something different. It felt like they were able to squeeze real life into their music - love, pain, happiness, yearning - not just three-minute songs to scale the pop charts. Their orchestration, melody, harmony, lyrical depth, how different and experimental everything sounded... One minute they're doing an intimate ballad, the next it's a song draped around an orchestra. They put a hook deep inside me that never left.

In junior high, I started amassing my own record collection. I still loved music for the harmony, melody, and rhythm, but now I was attracted to a different style of music. Bright, colorful new wave and punk rock coming from The Clash, Devo, The B52's, The Dead Kennedys and The Sex Pistols. I also devoured Van Halen, AC/DC, Supertramp, and Cheap Trick.

I was 15 years old when I got my first bass guitar in the summer of 1982. I would sit for hours in my room and play, practice, and invent sounds on it. My dad likes to say the moment I got that bass, I went into my room and didn't come out for seven years.

At some point, someone told me, "You should take some music lessons." I figured, yeah, that's what everybody does, right? You take music lessons.

My mom found a school nearby, and we gave it a shot. The guy was alright, but the lessons were terrible. He never asked me what I wanted, what I liked. I wanted to be like The Ramones, and these lessons were nothing close to that. They were formal, awkward, and uninspiring, which was the exact opposite of my experience listening to my favorite albums. It confused me. I didn't understand how music could be so powerful and colorful, and yet the lessons to learn how to play were so awful.

So I quit. I went home and realized that I just needed to learn about the records that I loved and learn how to apply what those musicians were playing to my own bass. And that's what I did. I learned from my records. I taught myself, and I learned about it because I loved it.

SEEING THE MATRIX

I never daydreamed of writing a "how to" book about playing bass and understanding modern music. I have always written, mostly tour journals that documented the ups and downs of my twenty-three years in Sugar Ray. I would scribble away in backstage rooms, hotels, tour buses, sober, hungover or half-drunk. These writings poured out of me to balance the insanity of the ride we were on. The only thing I had officially published were the liner notes from our *Greatest Hits* CD. Two whole pages!

How this book fell into place was partially from a YouTube channel I started in 2019. I was cranking out tutorials, Sugar Ray song breakdowns, and cover videos to help people like you learn to play bass. Even though I'd been playing bass for almost four decades, it wasn't until after I had created two hundred videos on YouTube that I was reminded how simple most songs were to learn and figure out. Over and over, it was presented to me in three parts - hundreds of songs. Some had four parts, some had two, but the majority seemed to be three.

There were nuances and different bits and pieces to corral the songs together, but it didn't matter; they were inevitably tied together by three parts. From Led Zeppelin to Taylor Swift, Foo Fighters to Elvis Presley, The Beatles to Ed Sheeran. Three parts.

I figured since this process was simple for me to see, maybe I could teach it to others? Then you wouldn't need me (in a good way), and you could learn what you wanted, when you wanted to learn it. If I could do that, show you this Three Part Method, the only thing left was to make sure you understood the basics of playing bass, so you have a solid foundation to build everything upon.

But how could I SHOW this process? Would it be a book or a video series? I wasn't sure. But I was excited. I was excited about the opportunity to teach something that could help you improve as a musician and help you rely on others less.

I realized it was a process, a way of SEEING songs as 3 parts, so I would call this process the Three Part Method.

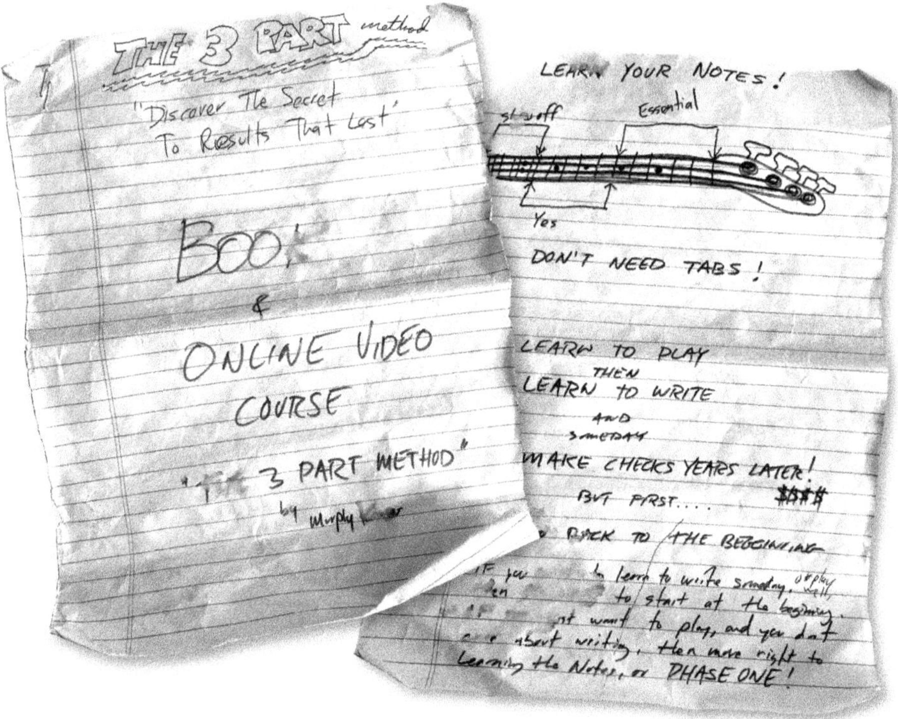

I created an outline in my yellow legal pad.

A few months into expanding that outline, it became clear it was a book.

If you choose to read this book and follow along with what I have laid out in terms of learning – the benefit to you is that you become more self-sufficient, and you will become a better bass player and musician. The challenge with videos, and the hours it takes to produce them, is that they teach one thing at a time. In contrast to that, this book offers you all the basics, from 40 years of experience, AND a method for learning that you can use forever, in one condensed manual.

Because of my experiences with complicated lessons when I was a kid, I was inspired to keep the instruction in this book as simple as possible. Think of this as a workbook. It's chronological, but you can jump around and find useful chapters as needed.

With that inspiration in mind, I'm going to show you how to understand your bass, how songs break into three parts, and how to glue everything together. I'm also going to ask what YOU like, where you get YOUR inspiration from, and we'll also cover a few things like confidence, understanding your role, sharing yourself, and understanding how important people are in your life.

I'm excited to dive in with you. I mean, not as excited as I was at Giants Stadium in front of 55,000 people. But still, pretty excited to help get you started.

CA
Fender

PHASE ONE:
LEARNING YOUR INSTRUMENT

01. WHAT IS A BASS?

Congratulations. You picked a cool instrument.

The bass is rad. It's rad because people underestimate it. Don't think it's true? I'll prove it to you. Has there ever been, in the history of the world, a kid who left a rock show, ears ringing, sweaty T-shirt, mind blown, fingers subconsciously playing air solos, who then turns to his friends, his dad or his weekend warrior uncle and announces, "I want to play **BASS!**"

No, there has not. Because it never happens. What is said though...

"I want to play **GUITAR!**"

Part of that is because nearly every stringed instrument can get lumped in as a guitar. Which is technically true. A bass is a bass guitar. But for some reason, the bass guitar can be somewhat unsexy to some. Like choosing to play the bassoon over the flute or clarinet in the orchestra. You get stuck with a bassoon, right? You don't often pick it.

Is it the same with a bass? Not for me. That was part of the charm. That everybody overlooked it – that everybody wanted to play guitar. Let them all pick the popular one. Let them all clamor at the overcrowded gates of the palatial estate of guitar, and I would head down the road to where there would be a bunch of funny-looking people hanging out at the thatched roof quirkiness of the bass shack. I can see the sign now. "COME ALL YEE WEARY OUTCASTS WITH BAD HAIRCUTS, CRAPPY PIANO TIE JACKETS, AND FAILED GUITARISTS... WE ACCEPT YOU HERE AT THE HOME OF BASS GUITAR..."

There I could hang out with my people. Other bassists!

But despite its deceptively narrow focus on playing the root of music and its limiting four strings, the bass has some powerful tricks up its sleeve. By being the root, the bottom end, the powerful foundation to modern music, you can make simple moves that have a deep impact on music. The bass can turn a chord on its head with just one note. We'll get to those moves later in the book.

Remember, although you play it one note at a time, one string at a time, that one little note is a huge, fat string that rumbles the wooden club stage, shaking the concrete foundation of the building it is built upon. I always did love that about bass. That it's an instrument you emit through other people's bodies, their chests, that it's something you feel, as opposed to something you hear. Overlooked, but subtly powerful in music, not a glory hound, AND the cousin to a bassoon? I'm in love.

Before we dive too deeply into roles, technique, and music common sense, let's look at what parts make up the modern electric bass.

You've got the **BODY** of your bass. It's attached to the **NECK**. The neck is usually bolted to the back of the body. Some basses are one piece, but they're expensive and not as common.

Bolt-on basses are great. They're what I play. The pickups sit in the middle of the **PICK GUARD**. The **PICK GUARD** is there to do exactly as advertised – to protect the bass body from getting all shredded by the strumming of your pick when you play. Plus, it looks cool, it breaks up the color of the body, and you can get some color combinations going if you want to customize your look.

- **VOLUME** and **TONE KNOB** do exactly as they say. One turns the volume up and down, the other controls the tone from a brighter and crisp sound (more treble) down to a more subtle and less-bright tone (more bass).

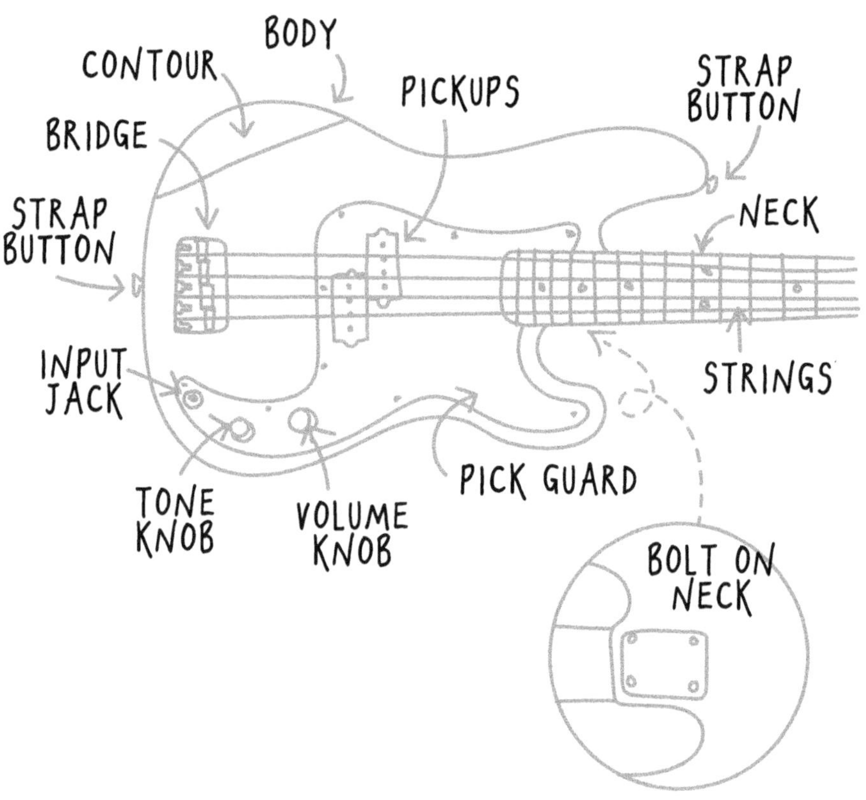

- **INPUT JACK** is where you plug in your instrument cable.

- **STRAP BUTTONS** are there so you can use a guitar strap and stand when you play.

- **BRIDGE** holds your strings and is mounted into the BODY of your bass.

- **STRINGS** run from your **BRIDGE** up the **NECK**, through the **NUT**, then into the **TUNING PEGS**.

- **TUNING PEGS** are on the **HEADSTOCK**. I've heard people call them **TUNING MACHINES**, **TUNING HEADS**, or **BASS TUNERS**.

- **NUT** is a little piece of plastic or graphite that keeps the strings in line as they go to the **TUNING PEGS**. It's a small detail on your bass that not many people talk about, but it's important to help maintain playability and tuning.

- **FRETS** are the metal pieces that break up the neck into different notes. The **FRET INLAYS** are decorative, but they offer a great cheat sheet of where you are on the neck. **INLAYS** are usually on the 3rd, 5th, 7th, 9th, and 12th frets. Yes, the inlays keep going higher (to 15th, 17th, and 19th), but I don't recommend playing up there. You'll find out why if you keep reading.

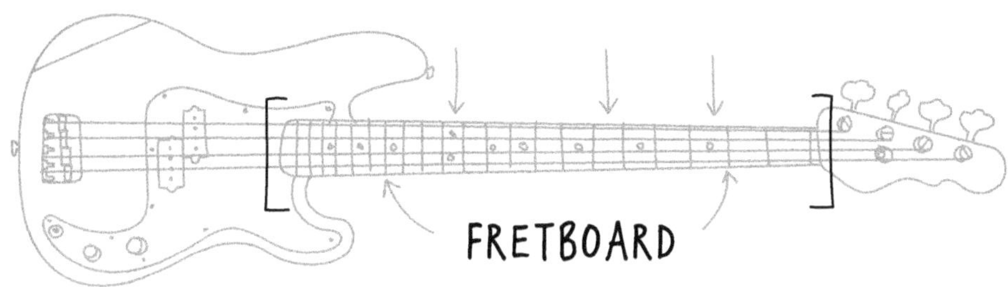

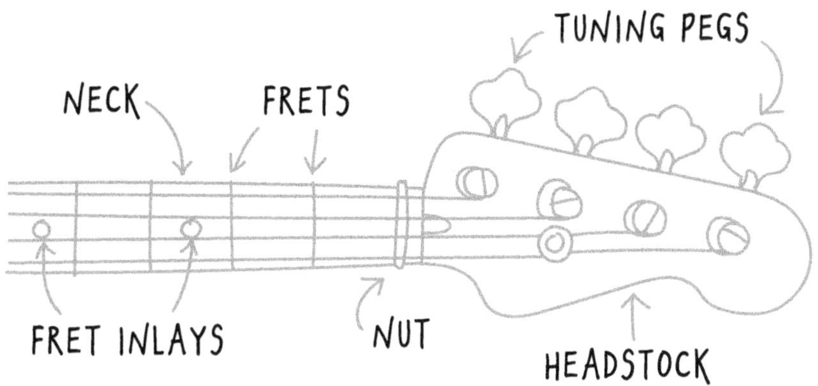

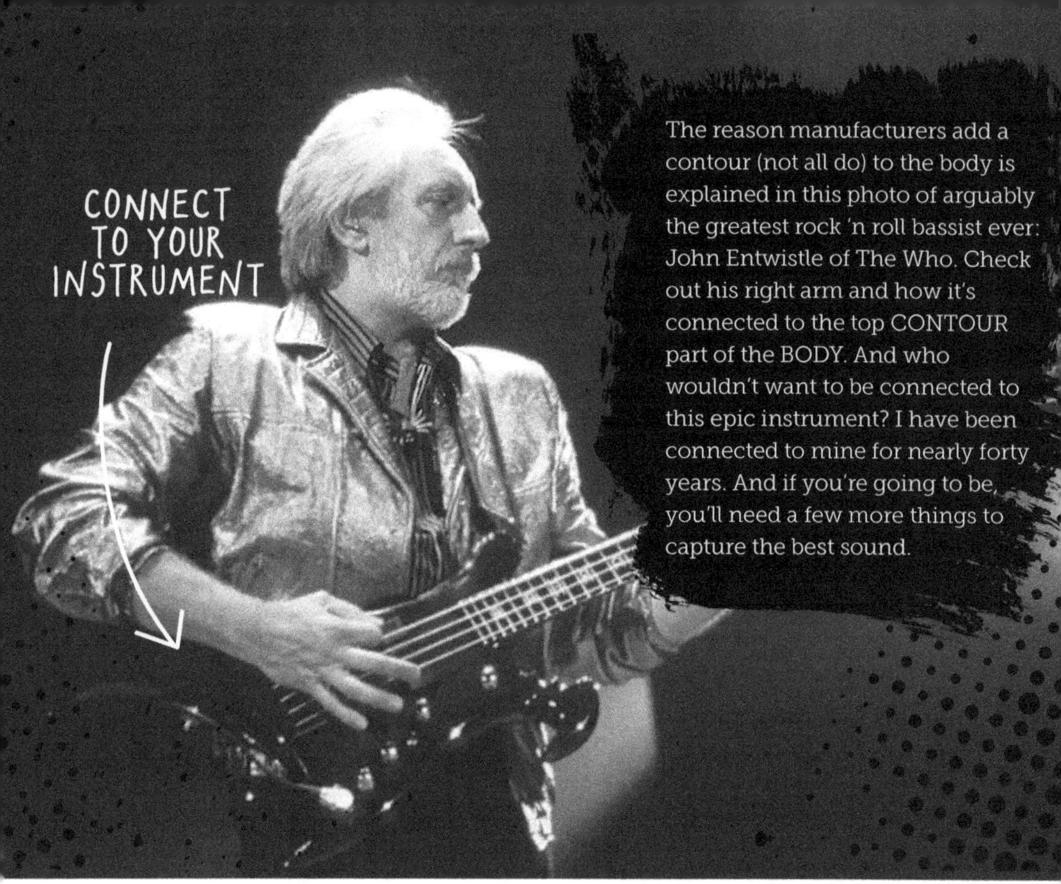

The reason manufacturers add a contour (not all do) to the body is explained in this photo of arguably the greatest rock 'n roll bassist ever: John Entwistle of The Who. Check out his right arm and how it's connected to the top CONTOUR part of the BODY. And who wouldn't want to be connected to this epic instrument? I have been connected to mine for nearly forty years. And if you're going to be, you'll need a few more things to capture the best sound.

There are five string basses. The 5th string adds a low 'B' string to the four strings to bring an even lower tone to playing. But I prefer four string basses. All my heroes played them so it's good enough for me. The **BODY** of the bass sometimes has a **CONTOUR** shaved into the top so that you can ground your right forearm onto it. It's important to connect to your instrument like this. You can see it better in the photo above.

02. BASS ACCESSORIES

Most instruments have accessories to make them rock, and the bass is no exception.

First, you'll need an **INSTRUMENT CABLE**. One end goes to your bass, the other end goes to whatever you want to send a signal to, which is usually an audio interface, an effects pedal, but most of the time it's an amplifier.

You'll need a **BASS AMP**. Basses are electric so you need to plug them in to hear them. (Thank you, Captain Obvious). I recommend the Fender Rumble series. It's great. It's light, easy to carry, and sounds loud and solid. There are so many brands and models. Just go to your nearest Guitar Center, Sam Ash, your local music shop, try out a bunch, and see which one you like. Or use Sweetwater and buy it online.

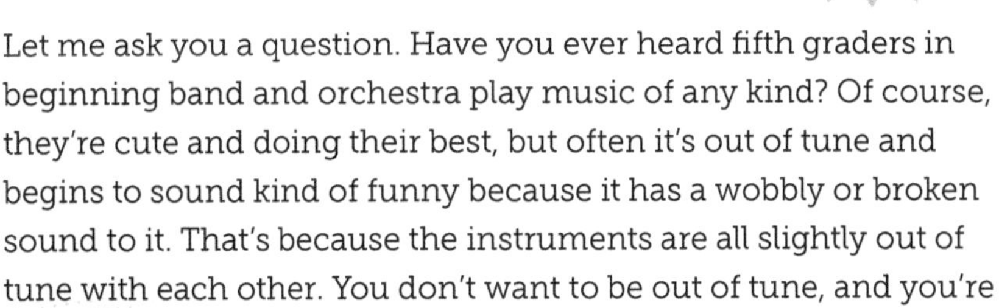

Let me ask you a question. Have you ever heard fifth graders in beginning band and orchestra play music of any kind? Of course, they're cute and doing their best, but often it's out of tune and begins to sound kind of funny because it has a wobbly or broken sound to it. That's because the instruments are all slightly out of tune with each other. You don't want to be out of tune, and you're not ten years old. Although if you are ten, and you're here, you are about to be the coolest kid in school. I recommend **SNARK TUNERS**. They're cheap, work well, and convenient. You just connect it to your headstock, tune up, then disconnect when you're ready to go.

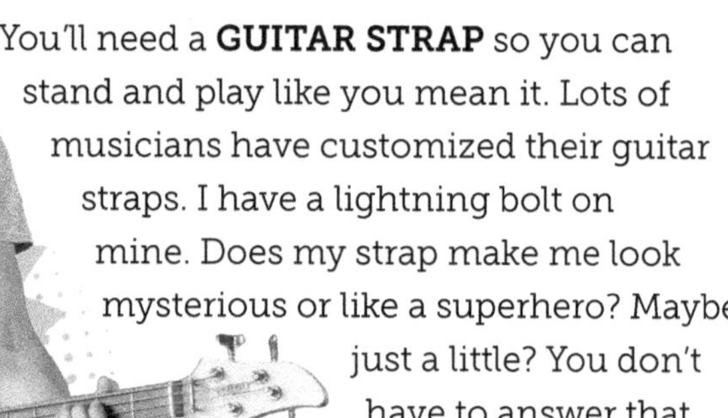

You'll need a **GUITAR STRAP** so you can stand and play like you mean it. Lots of musicians have customized their guitar straps. I have a lightning bolt on mine. Does my strap make me look mysterious or like a superhero? Maybe just a little? You don't have to answer that.

Whatever you do, just don't be like Double Strap Dan.

I get it, basses are heavy. But you're not lugging a piano around. You'll be fine without a harness.

The next accessory I recommend is for when you're NOT playing: a **GUITAR STAND**. They're inexpensive, and it shows that you take care of your axe (your bass). Not all musicians use them. Often on stage you'll see guitarists and bassists leaning their guitars up against things to rest. Don't do that. Get a proper guitar stand.

Finally, you'll need **STRINGS**. If your bass is new, you'll have the stock strings from the manufacturer. I'd recommend buying a new set. There's nothing like putting on a fresh set of strings.

The top brands are Ernie Ball, Rotosound, D'Addario, GHS, DR and La Bella. The two main kinds of bass strings are roundwounds and flatwounds. Roundwounds are a bit brighter, more modern, and the flatwounds are warmer, less top end, more old school Motown. I've always played roundwounds.

If a string company sponsors someone, they'll tell you those are the best. The truth? They're all pretty good. Rotosound has an impressive history of British legends who played their strings, and I've played GHS before with good results. I've used everything, but I've used Ernie Ball the most. Yes, they did sponsor me years ago, but they have a good reputation for a reason. They are priced fair, and they play and sound great. I recommend the Ernie Ball Slinkys.

Do your own research. Just pick one that's affordable for you... and has cool graphics. Why not?

03. LEARN YOUR NOTES & NECK

Notes are the foundation for everything in music. Every scale, every song, every tab, every key, from pop songs to orchestras, it's all about what notes you play, and often, what notes you don't play. Knowledge is power. If you learn where the notes on your neck are, you will be more confident when you play.

If I had my wish for you – it would be this:
1. Learn the **IMPORTANT NOTES** on your bass.
2. Learn **TWO SCALES**.
3. Learn what **OCTAVES** are.

That's it. If you learn those three things – important notes, two scales and octaves – then we're going to have a lot of fun.

GOT GPS?

Learning the notes on your bass is a little like learning the streets in your hometown. You know the streets where you live, right? I'm sure you do. It's good to know the important ones. The major routes. To work, school, market, the park, and home. You memorize them and never think about them again. They're ingrained. Same thing for your bass. You should know the major routes you'll use all the time.

Not every dark obscure alley and twisting road, but the high traffic areas. For some of you, however, the bass neck might look like a complete mess of frets, notes, strings, and confusion, and it might be intimidating to try to learn all those notes on your bass.

The good news is that learning
notes on your bass isn't hard. It just
takes time, some patience, and
repetition. The even better news is
that you don't have to learn every
note, not even close. I don't know
all mine and I've been playing for
four decades.

If you learn the notes like I mentioned,
your comprehension will increase, you'll
understand more of what you're doing, and
you'll probably have more fun.

I will talk about **TABS** in this book. If you don't know what tabs are,
they're like a cheat sheet for learning songs. What they do is show
you, one by one, where your fingers go for the entire song.
They're easy to use, save time, and they help you play the song
right. The one thing they don't do, in my opinion, is help you
understand your fretboard or the **NOTES** you're playing, because
you're just following numbers.

When you learn the **NOTES**, you're taking the lead, and you're
not letting someone tell you what to do. Tabs don't leave anything
open to interpretation. Learning notes does. Learning and
comprehending what you're playing also opens a place in your
brain that starts working on decision making, improvisation, and
collaboration.

Let me use an analogy to further illustrate the difference between
tabs and notes... Let's say you want to sketch a bald eagle. If you
are using **TABS**, you would have a dotted line along the edge of
the Eagle to show you where to sketch. If you are learning your
NOTES, you would have to go into the wild, or to a zoo, and
look at an Eagle up close, and study them so you can sketch
from memory.

In a perfect world, you would use both. Tabs for when you need it quick, and learning your notes for when you have time to study so you can comprehend more of what is happening on your fretboard.

In the coming pages, you will learn where the important notes are on the neck, and I'll be breaking them down in 3 places.

1. ESSENTIAL
2. OK
3. SHOW OFF

A QUICK WORD ON FRETS

Frets are the metal things that divide your fretboard. When someone says, "Fret 5," they don't mean the actual metal fret. They mean the gap right after fret 5. So technically, they mean "Gap 5" (see below).

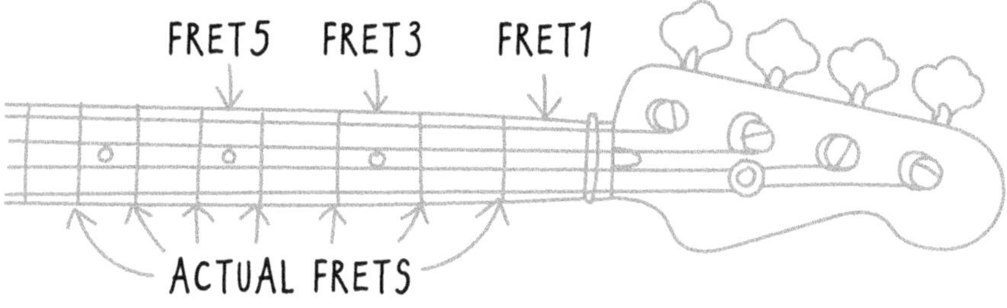

DISCLAIMER ALERT! I said 'music common sense' earlier in this chapter because I only want to teach you simple music concepts. Theory, in my experience, can go too deep, and it starts to get more confusing than it needs to be, or at least for me. I won't go too deep and teach you things you don't need. I'll just stick to the basics.

TUNING

I recommend using an electronic tuner to tune your bass strings (see page 15). They're affordable, easy to use, and **FUN**! It's like a video game!

To tune your bass, just attach the tuner to your headstock, and play an open "G" string (The "G" is the smallest string). Let it ring, making sure no other strings are ringing, and the tuner will then show you what **NOTE** your string is at. All you do now (video game skills at the ready), is use your **TUNING PEGS** to raise or lower the pitch until you successfully see a "G" on the tuner. See, I told you, it's a video game.

That's it. That's the process I use. Once you get your smallest string to read out "G" on the tuner, then move onto the other strings: D, A, and E.

A tip – Don't rush it. Let the string "ring" for a bit so the tuner can accurately "hear" the pitch of your string and give you a correct reading.

04. THE ESSENTIAL NOTES

Looking down at your bass, there are a lot of notes. The good news is that you only need to learn a handful of them. And here's even better news – there are only **SEVEN** total notes on your bass.

SEVEN? You might say to me. How that can be? Well, it's true. The number of notes isn't the hard part. It's memorizing where they are – since they're spread out – that takes some work. But I'm positive **YOU CAN DO THIS!** I'll show you the way…

We're going to start on the **ESSENTIAL NOTES**: frets 0–5. You can play thousands of songs if you master this simple area of your bass.

To begin, you should know the open strings: E, A, D, G. The strings are also numbered, and you count them from the bottom, starting on G, and count upwards. The G string is 1, the D string is 2, the A string is 3, and the E string is 4.

It helps when you're learning to play the note to *say it out loud*. Say it and play it.

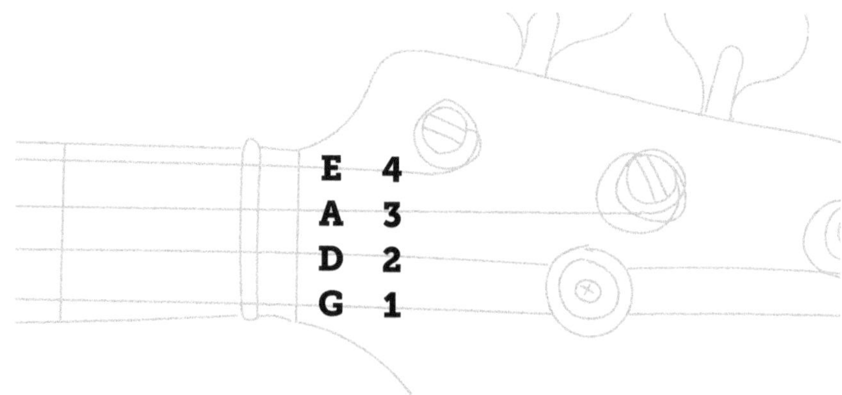

Now let's get to the essential notes on the fretboard. We will start with the top half.

This TOP HALF of the ESSENTIAL NOTES are the bread and butter of your bass.

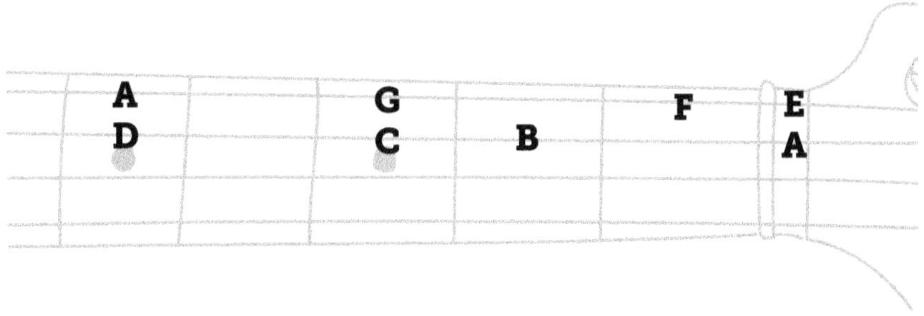

The crème de la crème. This is where you get paid. Thousands of songs are within these 8 notes. You could learn just these 8 notes and skip to Chapter 7 if you wanted. But stick around. It's music, not algebra. It's fun to learn this stuff.

All the notes from Sugar Ray's songs "Fly," "Every Morning" and "Someday" are here. ALL OF THEM. Not a single note from these songs sits *OUTSIDE* this top 8. That's crazy, right? Meaning, I do not have to move my hand from this area to play every hit we have. When I was a kid, I would have been STOKED to know those notes were all I needed to learn.

INSIGHT: Practice learning these notes in a loop. Think of the alphabet, and just play up the alphabet. If you start on D, then your next note is E, and go until you hit D again. Start on A, B is next, then loop around until you hit A. Repeat this. Play the alphabet and say each note as you play it. It will help ingrain the notes.

Now let's turn to the bottom half.

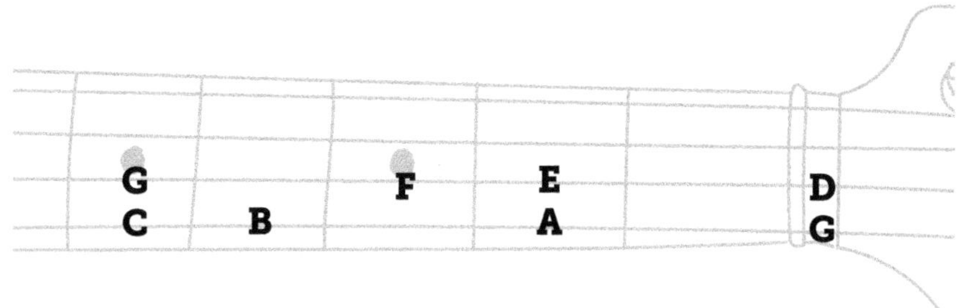

Same looping method here. Since there are only 7 notes (*spoiler alert - there are sharps and flats, more on them later), there are a lot of the same notes from the **TOP HALF** just repeating down here.

But how do we find them? The answer is something called **OCTAVES**. Octaves are when the note just repeats in a higher (or lower) place. The way they repeat is through **SCALES**. Scales are a way the 7 notes are arranged. And when you hit the 8th note, that's an octave.

Here are all the **ESSENTIAL NOTES**, crammed together for you to see and recap.

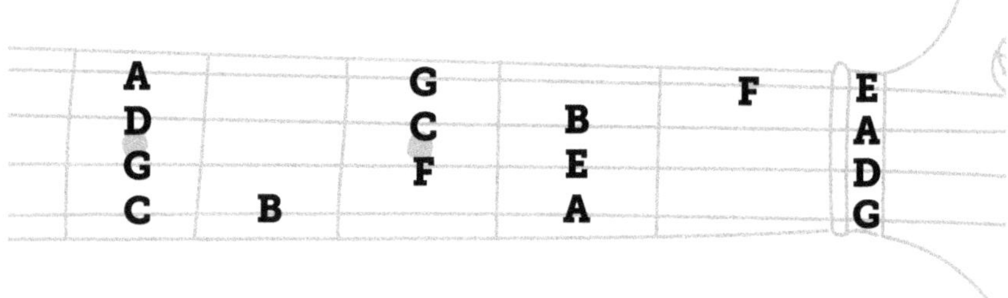

Do you see any patterns? Take another look.

Let me show you the patterns (or octaves) I see when I play bass.

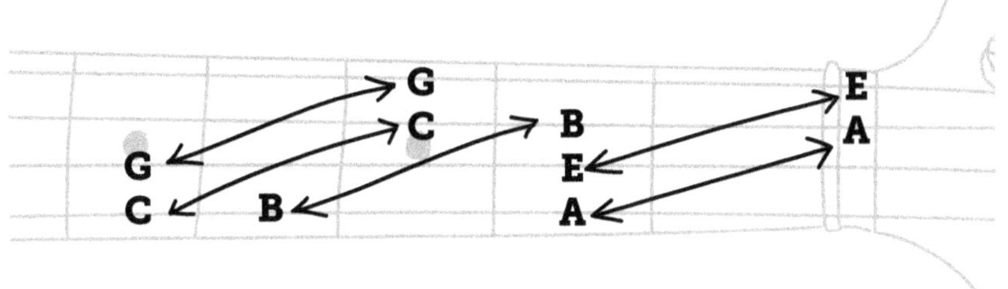

And the cool thing is that this pattern doesn't just happen here. It happens all over the neck, anywhere you find a note. It's all this connected.

OCTAVES ARE COOL

Octaves are cool. You can use them to add dimension to what you're playing on bass because when you go up an octave, you increase energy. (Higher notes generally add energy or intensity). You can't go wrong because it's the same note, so it's not risky. They're great to add dynamics and power, but they also help you "see" your fretboard better.

They do this because when you read and learn about Major Scales in Chapter 7, you'll learn that Octaves are the beginning and ending notes in any scale. So wherever you are, you'll know the beginning and ending of any scale.

Examples of octaves in classic songs:
"Immigrant Song" – The main riff in this Zeppelin classic is based on octave patterns.
"Tom Sawyer" – The opening notes in this Rush song are an E octave, as well as later uses of octave patterns.
"Bulls on Parade" – Great riff from Rage Against The Machine. Octaves. Both guitar and bass.
"My Sharona" – A classic, timeless riff. Octaves, from The Knack.
"All Apologies" – Drop D but Krist Novaselic is still using octaves to anchor the low end in this Nirvana song.

"Higher Ground " – In this Stevie Wonder cover from the Red Hot Chili Peppers, Flea is using octaves in the opening bassline. A very common technique for slap bass.

Here's another way to look at how notes (or octaves) are connected.

Octaves, and seeing how they connect on your fretboard, are an important tool for learning where two notes are at any given time on your bass, doubling the amount of information you can have.

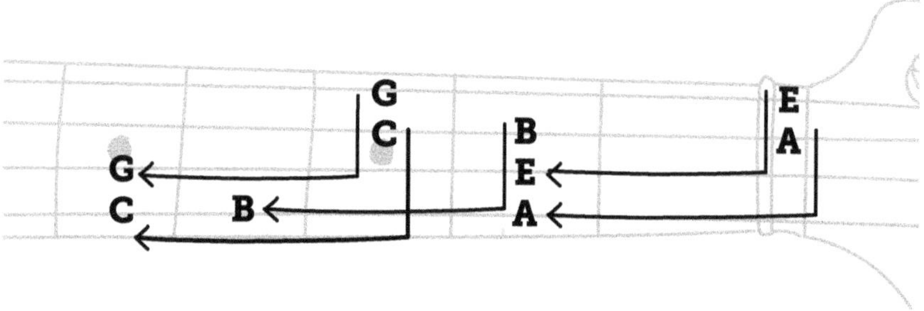

Here are the 7 **ESSENTIAL NOTES** on a piano keyboard.

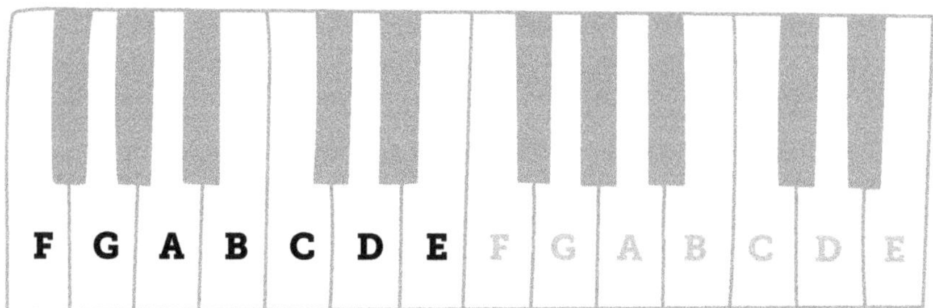

ACTION STEPS

1. After practicing the essential notes, see if you can close your book, iPhone, or computer screen, and play the **TOP HALF** by memory. If you get it, move on to playing the **BOTTOM HALF** by memory.

2. Go back and listen to those songs I mentioned that have classic riffs based on octaves. Get inspired! Crank up the music... and try to make up your own octave riff. Record it onto your phone. Play it back and listen.

05. THE YES NOTES

Now that you've dug into the **ESSENTIAL NOTES**, it's time for more. It's time for you to dig into the **YES NOTES** area.

YES NOTES are anything between the 6th and 11th frets. Even though you can play a thousand songs down low in the **ESSENTIAL** area, you don't always want to stay there. If you want to change it up, playing in the 6-11 fret range helps push the energy higher.

While the **ESSENTIAL NOTES** are the anchor of your bass, the **YES NOTES** are the flavor creators. When you go up higher on your bass, you bring up the intensity. You also add warmth when you play high notes. So many classic basslines use this area to provide pop when it's needed. Paul Simonon's bass in "London Calling" slides up here to match the angst and rebelliousness of the song's message. If you have never heard this classic, put down this book for three minutes and twenty-two seconds and listen to the bassline.

Let's say you need to play a high E note. Playing it on the D string, second fret, there's not a lot of meat on the bone for that position. It will sound a little bit weak because the D string is the second smallest string on your guitar. Instead, how about we shift to the A string and play it there?

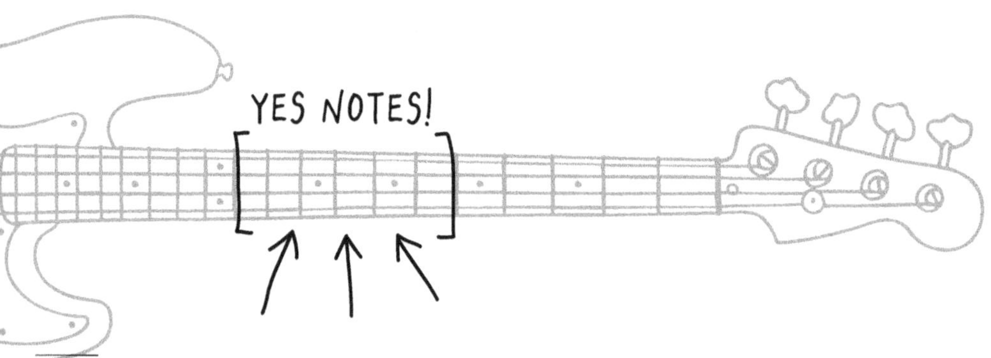

Check the diagram above. Both are E notes. The one on the right is in the **ESSENTIAL** zone, bottom half, and the other is in the **YES** zone. Play them both. Listen to what they sound like, and how they feel different to you.

The reason that A string E sounds beefier than the D string is because the A string is beefier. Simple, right? I almost don't know of a situation where you'd want to play a note that has less depth to it. So if I want low, I'm in the **ESSENTIAL**, and if I want high, I slide up to the **YES** zone.

More mass = bigger note. That's why playing notes in the **YES** range is a great idea when you require more energy.

LET'S COMPARE TWO OTHER NOTES...
Play the 2nd fret on the G String. That's an A. Listen to it. Okay, now play the 7th fret of the D string.

Do they sound different to you?

For me, I LOVE the A on the 7th fret of the D string. I play that A all the time. The other one, not so much.

I play that 7th fret A for the verse of our song "Answer the Phone." The progression goes A, E, F#,D. It does it 4 times in the verse, and I play that 7th fret A every time in the verse. The chorus has the

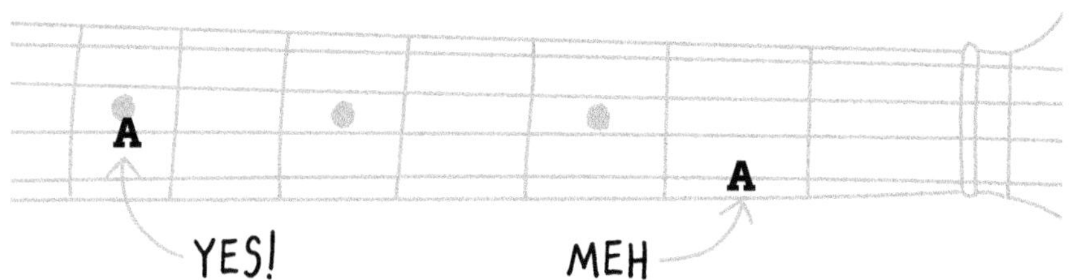

same notes as the verse – it doesn't change – but the intensity ramps up in the chorus, and so I play the open A string to bring more loudness and add bottom end. I used to add an overdrive pedal as well to really take it over the top. So that's an example of how you can use the same notes in different parts of your bass to match up the intensity.

HOW ABOUT ANOTHER COMPARISON...

The B note on the 7th fret of the E string is a classic. So big and warm. Try it against its counterpart on the 2nd fret of the A string.

ANOTHER ONE...

Try the F# way up on the 9th fret, A string. Love that little sonovabitch. Sounds so good. Way different than the F# on the 4th fret of the D string. Try them and see for yourself. What do they sound like to you?

Or maybe you'll see it differently and create your own opinions.

Remember, it's a toy, a canvas. Play around. Have fun.

Remember, the **YES** zone is where you can play higher notes if you want to push the intensity or have it sound a little warmer, a little beefier than their high counterparts in the **ESSENTIAL** zone.

ACTION STEPS

1. Play the same note, but in two different areas. What does it sound like? How are they different?

2. Play a song one way – then play it again but play the notes in different positions. Does it change? Why do you think it changes? Which way works better?

One of our very first shows in
Europe. The crowd was huge,
and we were all so happy to
be there, we were absolutely
floating onstage. I have no
good explanation as to why
I wore soccer shorts. Oh yeah,
it was the 90's!

06. THE SHOWOFF ZONE

Don't even think about it. You don't need to be way up here. Think of it like a bad part of town, and mom warned you about going there. You're a bass player, act like it. Don't act like a guitar player. Bassists do their job; we hold down the bottom end, and then we pack up our shit and go home.

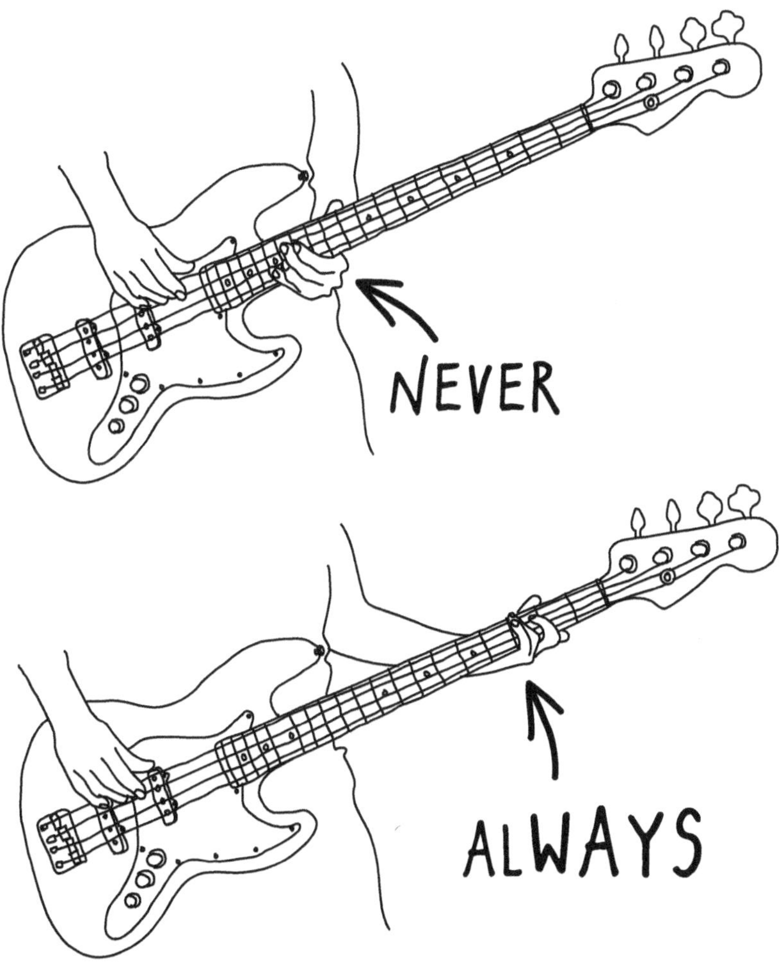

I DO NOT WANT YOU venturing way up beyond the state line, which is the 12th fret. You **NEVER*** need to be up there, so just forget it. The only time I ever go up there is maybe at the end of a song, and I'm getting all crazy in the root key, just making a ton of noise. But I'll only do that for a moment. I'll quickly get my ass back down to where I belong. 3rd fret. 5th fret, open string; something like that. Think blue collar. You aren't white collar, you're a bassist. Dig it. Love it.

Even on "Dazed & Confused," where John Paul Jones plays that iconic bass line way up high, he only goes up to the 10th fret on the A string. "Under Pressure," probably my favorite song of all time and one of the greatest songs ever written, starts on the 12th but never goes above it.

If you can write a song like that, go for it. Otherwise, hold down the bottom end in the **ESSENTIAL** or **YES** zone and make your band members happy.

***Obvious overly dramatic warning**
My point about this isn't to *never* go up into the showoff zone, rather, it's that you'll earn most of your keep playing down in the essential zone. Of course, you can go wherever you want. There are no rules. Make up your own. These are mine.

Look at this photo – where is Flea playing? He's jamming right inside the **ESSENTIAL NOTES** area. Except for a couple specific needs to go up high, you can rest assured you'll never need to play up there.

07. POSTURE & HAND POSITIONS

Standing or sitting? Gripping or holding? You decide.

Before we move onto learning a few scales, I wanted to talk about how you hold the bass when you are playing or practicing. When you're sitting down and playing bass, (if you're right-handed like me) your bass will sit on your right leg.

As you can see, the bass is sitting, from its lower cutout area, on my right leg, and my hands are ready to play. I'm using both hands to play the strings, to make the sounds I want.

If you want to stand up and practice, add your guitar strap and adjust the height to what is comfortable. Here is an example of me standing and playing bass.

Part of the reason I didn't like music lessons when I was a kid was because the guy wanted me to hold my left hand like this **ALWAYS**.

Ever try holding your hand like that for a long time? It sucks! It's exhausting, but more importantly, it's unnecessary. I understand why he wanted me to hold my hand like that. It's because it does make it easier to play some notes, because with your hand more underneath the neck, it makes it easier to reach certain notes.

But the truth is, your hand **NEEDS TO MOVE** around when you play. It shouldn't ever be stuck in one position.

SOME EXAMPLES OF MY HAND MOVING AROUND WHEN I PLAY

HERE'S ANOTHER ANGLE

As you can see, my hand is moving all over the place. My thumb sometimes disappears, and then sometimes it's flying **OVER THE TOP FOR A SLAM DUNK!** Well, not a slam dunk, but it does appear to be flying over the top of the neck and fretboard. **THAT'S GOOD.** Let yourself move freely for whatever is needed for you to play something.

Check out these two photos that show how much the position of your thumb and hand will change.

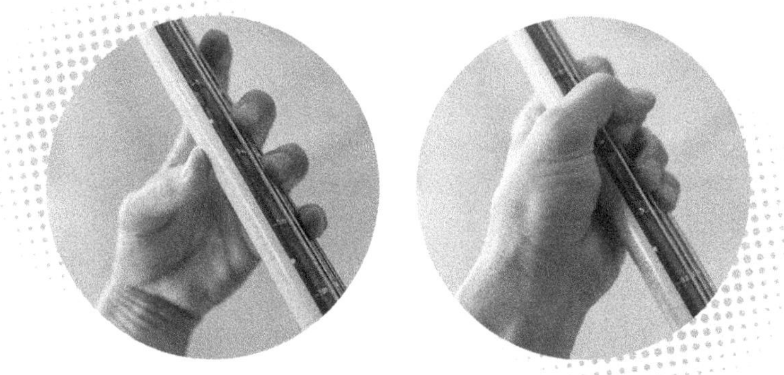

Regarding your **RIGHT HAND** (or vice versa if you are left-handed), if you are playing with your fingers, I want to make sure you are naturally letting your right forearm rest on top of your bass.

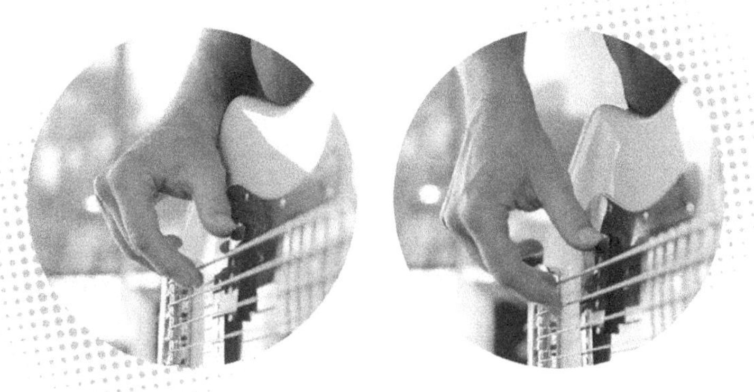

Of course, there are exceptions, and your arm will **NEED** to move away from your bass sometimes, but I want you to be relaxed when you play and remind you that being grounded to something is good. So lay it on there. Get cozy with the body of your bass.

Holding a pick is simple. Just grab it how you'd like. Here's how I do it.

I'm not even aware of it (the best way), but as you can see, I'm grounding my right forearm into the bass. Again, I don't just LEAVE it there, I am free to move, but I'm generally using my forearm to ground myself into it so I can play hard, sound good, and keep good timing and rhythm.

HOW HARD DO YOU PLAY ON THE STRINGS?

I once heard a story from a guitar tech I met on the road who said that AC/DC's Angus Young played with a very light touch on his strings. I was like – say what? I thought from all his antics and physicality onstage, that he might play with a heavy hand. The truth is, Angus, or you, should play for what fits your band, your songs, whether it's a light touch, or a heavy hand.

When we used to play "Answer the Phone" in Sugar Ray, I'd have red pick shavings all over my pick guard after that song because I played it so hard with a pick. loved playing that song. But I didn't play "Fly," "Someday," and "Every Morning" that way. Those were our more mellow radio songs. I played those with a lighter touch.

ONE MORE THING
Your left hand, traditionally, has numbers that correspond to each finger. I have no idea why. I suppose sometimes you want to tell someone to play a note with "THAT" finger, and by having a numbers system, you know which finger you're talking about.

Here's how the numbers go.

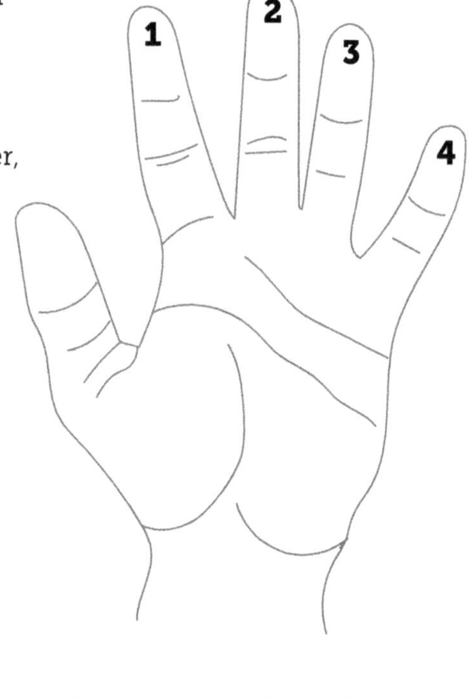

OR IF YOU LIKE...

JACK JOHNSON

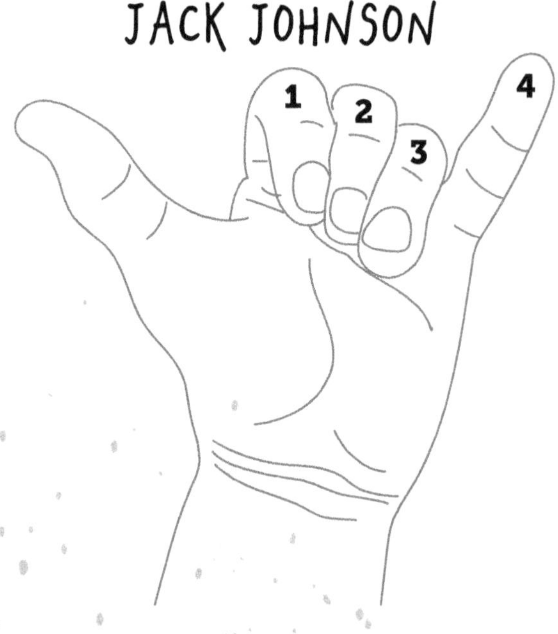

METALLICA

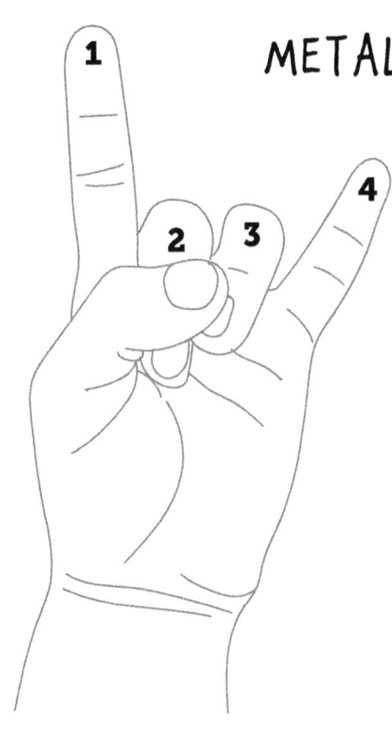

GETTING CUT OFF ON THE HIGHWAY

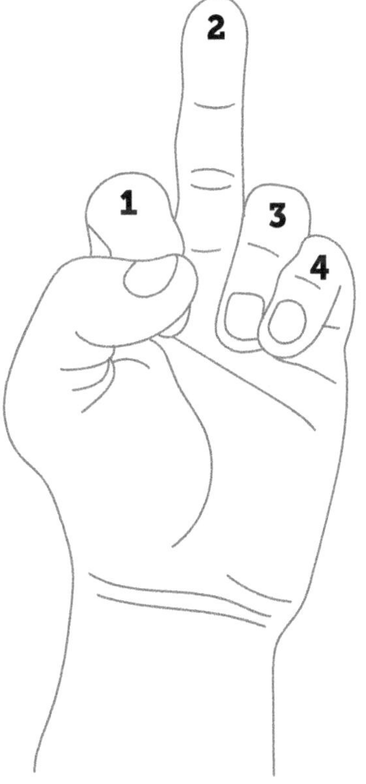

08. THE MAJOR SCALE

"Whaa? But you said no confusing complicated stuff…"

I won't be trying to teach you advanced scales and modes and all kinds of confusing things. I stated my case that you don't need deep theory if you're not interested. However, I will be showing you a few simple scales that will help you understand things better, which is always cool. So let me jump into a tiny bit right now: **Scales are a series of notes that help make the building blocks of chords and songs.**

Scales are important, but not so you can play them. I've been playing live gigs for nearly 35 years, all over the world, and never once did I play a Major scale in front of a crowd. Not on its own. But I know how to play it, and I know what it sounds like. Therefore, I know what it does. I'd like you to know, too.

First off, regarding the sound of scales:
- Major scales sound "happy" or like a blue-sky day.
- Minor scales sound "sad" or like an overcast or rainy day.

Kinda weird, right? And why is that? Why should scales sound different? I'll get into why scales sound the way they do **BECAUSE OF INTERVALS** in the next chapter, and how the Major and minor differ. (Always write Major with a capitol "M" and minor with a lowercase "m".)

For now, *we're focused on learning the Major scale*. This is a great first scale to learn because so many songs we know, and love, are built from it.

If we jump right into the notes on your bass, starting on the low E string, it goes like this.

THE 'A' MAJOR SCALE

The traditional way to start it is by playing the 'A' on the 5th fret, 4th string, then just walk the alphabet to B, C#, D, E, F#, G#, then finally A. There are only 7 notes here. The A is played twice. Those two A's are called an **OCTAVE**. Octaves are cool. I play those suckers all the time live and on records.

That's it. That's the A Major scale.

Let's look at it slowly, one more time, but we'll add the numbers of the scale with each note.

'A' MAJOR WITH NUMBERS

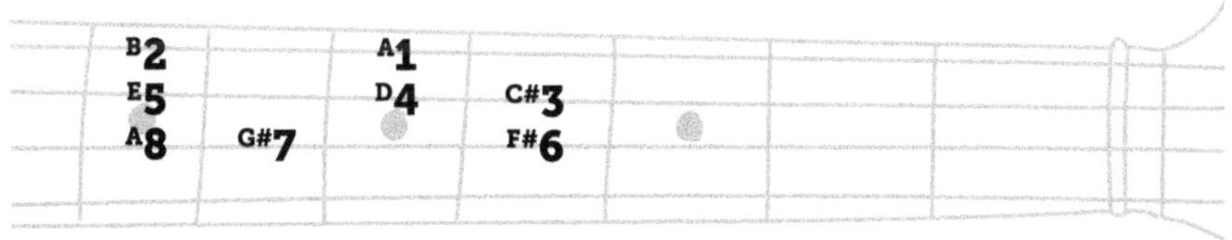

All you have to do is memorize this shape. If you can do that, then you can play the notes of Major scales all over your bass. *This exact shape repeats everywhere*. For instance, if you slide this shape up **two steps**, the note sitting at #1 will now be a B, and this same configuration will repeat for a Major scale for B, but with different notes, of course.

Remember I said I never just stood in front of a crowd and played an A Major scale, up and down? Because that would kind of be like playing "Chopsticks" if you were Elton John to a packed Dodger Stadium. Well, Elton might do it to be funny, or ironic, but again, the real reason you learn it is so that you can understand how music connects. Chords are the lifeblood that keeps music interesting and colorful and how music fits together.

SCALES BECOME CHORDS

Okay, so I just told you that *scales are a series of notes that help make the building blocks of chords and songs*.

Why? And how do they do this? Let's dig into the **HOW** right now. Buckle up...

Major and minor scales are the building blocks to songs because **they make up the notes of a particular chord**. Yes, that's right. If you play an A Maj chord on piano (there are many ways to do this), you're only playing the notes of the A Maj scale.

But don't just jump over to a piano and play an A Maj chord with a B in it. It'll sound like crap. But I thought I just said scales make up the notes of chords? I did, just not every note. That's because some notes are **MORE IMPORTANT** than others for that chord to sound right.

In my version of music theory, I call the more important notes **DOMINANT**, and I call the other notes **PASSING**. Here's what I mean by Dominant and Passing. Again, they are my theories. Don't go rushing to your music teacher talking about 'passing' notes, they might look at you funny and flunk you. To me, **DOMINANT** notes are the big, important ones, and the **PASSING** notes are the ones that you use lightly and only in certain moments. Passing notes connect the dots, but they don't lay the foundation.

GRILLIN' STEAKS

Let me explain it with food. In this case, the dinner is the song, and the individual items are the chords. So the individual items make up the dinner, just like the chords make up the song.

For example, let's say you're making dinner, and you're grilling steaks. With that steak dinner, you'll probably include a starch, maybe baked potatoes, or French Fries, also some greens, maybe green beans, or asparagus. While the whole thing makes up your overall dinner (i.e., the song), the steaks, green beans, and fries are the chords that pull that dinner together. That's what chords do. They color the songs and give them more flavor. Same with the meat, starches, and vegetables. It colors your dinner, gives it balance.

Now going deeper, let's get to the ingredients to make the steak tasty, which would also be the notes of an 'A' **MAJOR SCALE**. Remember they were **A, B, C#, D, E, F#, G#**.

Okay, so your steak ingredients (or notes) look like this:
Steaks
Sauce
Salt
Pepper
Crispy onions
Butter
Blue cheese (FYI the dude who edited my book advised to take blue cheese out, but no chance, brother.)

I'm hungry already. Maybe I should go eat. No, no. I'm going to focus. Back to the meal / song.

So now you've got your stuff ready to make a fantastic steak. The way I look at it, there are some things that will be more important on this list. Obviously, the steaks themselves are the most important. They're the **TONIC**, or **KEY**, or **DOMINANT** note here.

But let's add the others.

Since most chords are made up of just three notes (aka a **TRIAD**),
I have to pick two ingredients to add to the steak. To me, the other
two most important ingredients to add a great steak are butter
and salt.

So, there's my triad. Steak, butter, and salt.

You could cook **with just those ingredients**, and it would be good.
So those are my **DOMINANT** notes.

But to connect the dinner even further, I want to add some other
flavors. Let's add crispy onions, blue cheese, pepper, and sauce.
I wouldn't base my steak on those flavors or add them in massive
doses; I would just use them sparingly to add to the dinner. Same
with certain notes of a scale. I mentioned the "B" not vibing in the
"A" chord. That's because the "B," like the blue cheese or crispy
onions are best just added in lightly.

DO YOU REALLY WANT TO GO DEEPER?

If we wanted to go even a bit deeper, we could go into what makes up a **TRIAD**. Triads are the most common way to play a chord on the piano. Triads are made up, usually, of the 1st note, 3rd note, and 5th note of a scale. That would be A, C#, E. Or, Steak, Salt, Butter.

Can you pick out the Triad here?

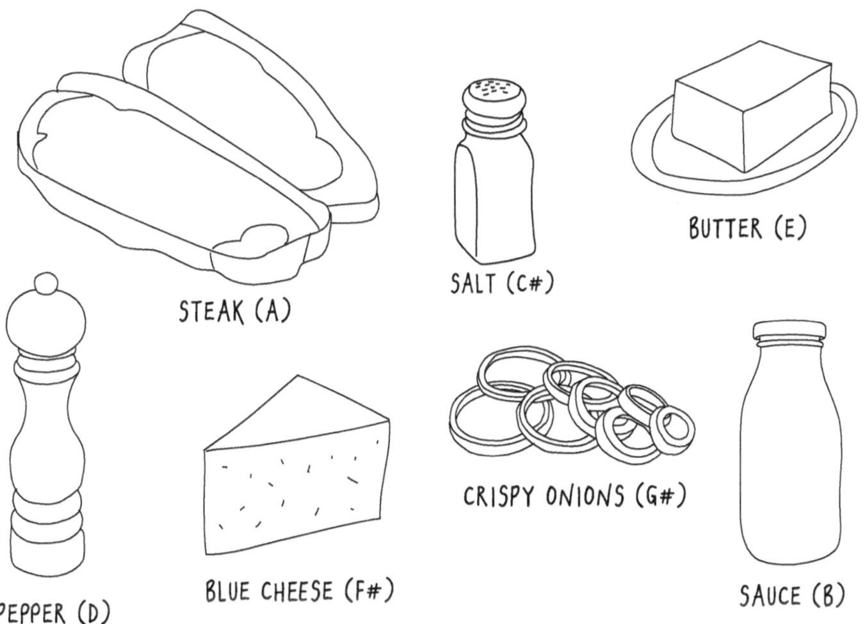

TRADITIONAL MUSIC THEORY			MURPHY'S WAY OF SEEING IT		
1. THE STEAKS	A	TONIC	1. THE STEAKS	A	DOMINANT (OR TONIC)
2. SAUCE	B	SUPERTONIC	2. SAUCE	B	PASSING
3. SALT	C#	MEDIANT	3. SALT	C#	DOMINANT
4. PEPPER	D	SUBDOMINANT	4. PEPPER	D	PASSING
5. BUTTER	E	DOMINANT	5. BUTTER	E	DOMINANT
6. BLUE CHEESE	F#	SUBMEDIANT	6. BLUE CHEESE	F#	PASSING
7. CRISPY ONIONS	G#	LEADING TONE	7. CRISPY ONIONS	G#	PASSING

See how hard they make it?

My way of seeing this is that the dominant notes make up simple chords that I can use. That's as deep as I want to go. Their way is that the Tonic, Supertonic, Mediant, Subdominant, etc. all help you go deeper and deeper into an abyss that I just frankly get a headache thinking about.

That's why I like the dinner example. Who doesn't like a great steak?! Some notes (ingredients) are dominant; some are passing. But they all help make the steak (chord) taste right so that the dinner (song) can strike the right balance and come together for the best possible experience. (Sorry, vegetarians – this could also apply to some delicious cauliflower or fresh spinach or seasoned rice or... well, you get the idea)

Work on the shape of that Major scale. And remember, it's the happy scale. Either go play it somewhere that you love, or just let the sound of it bring you there. While dreaming of a steak dinner of course. Bon appetit!

Some examples of Major scale songs:
Here Comes the Sun – The Beatles (A Major)
Perfect – Ed Sheeran (Ab Major)
Bohemian Rhapsody – Queen (Bb Major)
Can't Help Falling in Love – Elvis Presley (D Major)
Sittin' On the Dock of A Bay – Otis Redding (F Major)
I Walk the Line – Johnny Cash (D Major)
Rocket Man – Elton John (C Major)
You Shook Me All Night Long – AC/DC (G Major)
Friends in Low Places – Garth Brooks (A Major)
Should I Stay or Should I Go? – The Clash (D Major)
Wish You Were Here – Pink Floyd (G Major)
My Best Friend – Queen (C Major)
Fly – Sugar Ray (A Major)
Isn't She Lovely – Stevie Wonder (E Major)
Like A Rolling Stone – Bob Dylan

ACTION STEPS

1. Play the scale, starting on any note you like. Say the notes as you move around.

2. When jamming to a simple song, say Bob Dylan's "Knockin' on Heaven's Door," (which is in G Major) start walking your bass around using the G Major scale, and see if you can connect how the song moves by using the 7 notes of the G Major scale.

3. Make yourself a nice streak dinner using my (or your) ingredients and pay attention to how you use them. What were your dominant ones? What were your passing ones?

09. THE MINOR SCALE

I love the minor scale. I love it because it sounds sad, or melancholy.

Where the Major scale sounds like a blue-sky day and everything is going your way, the minor scale sounds like a rainy day or an uneasy situation. I don't know why I like that, but I do. To me, the minor scale seems to hold more opportunity for topics. When you're happy, it's just one thing. You're good. But with sadness, the degrees to which you could explore your themes open wider. For me, anyway.

Let's look at the A minor scale. Obviously, it's a little different from the Major scale. Can you spot the difference?

THE 'A' MINOR SCALE

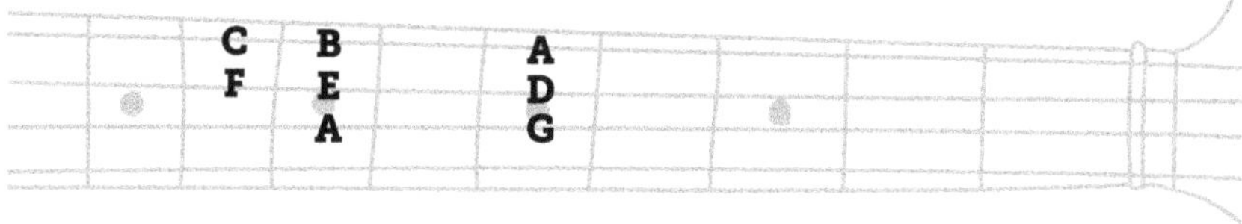

Just like the Major scale, practice by playing the alphabet. Start anywhere, play the next note going up, and go in a loop. Play it forwards, backwards, and have fun. I'm not interested in you shredding the minor scale. I can't play it fast. That's not the point. Speed doesn't always equal emotion. But I DO want you to understand the feel and sound of it.

Let's do the minor scale AGAIN. **This time I'll add the numbers of the scale**. It's important to learn the numbers, so practice saying the number as you go.

09

'A' MINOR WITH NUMBERS

THE REASON WHY SCALES CAN SOUND DIFFERENT

The reason why scales can sound different, or happy, or sad, is the distance between the notes, or the **INTERVALS**.

You can attempt to play one note with a lot of emotion, like B.B. King did, bending it and sustaining it, but it's still just one note. Only so much you can do. When you introduce another note, AH-HA! That's when you can really convey emotion and tweak how you want it to sound - by altering the distance between notes.

Let's try it.

On a piano, or keyboard, play one note, let it ring, and then play another note very close to it. Find a distance that sounds creepy, uneven, or dissonant. Now find a different starting note. Play it and find another note that blends with it better. Find something smooth sounding. Listen to them ring together, just two notes. What does it sound like to you? It shouldn't sound dissonant or uneasy. It should sound solid, powerful, or connected. That's one way to create emotion from music. Varying the distance between two notes, and using either the tension, or the harmony between notes to create the feeling you are looking for.

Music is emotion. Learning what a minor scale *looks like and sounds like* will help you understand how to convey emotion in your own playing and help you understand how the intervals between notes can change the color of your music.

Experiment. Have fun with it. Mess around on your bass.

Some examples of minor scale songs:

Hotel California – Eagles (A minor)

Stairway to Heaven – Led Zeppelin (A minor)

Ain't No Sunshine – Bill Withers (A minor)

Unforgiven – Metallica (A minor)

Californication – Red Hot Chilli Peppers (A minor)

Heart of Gold – Neil Young (E minor)

All Along the Watchtower – Jimi Hendrix (A minor)

Wonderwall – Oasis (F# minor)

House of the Rising Sun – The Animals (A minor)

Black Magic Woman – Santana (D minor)

Chop Suey! – System of a Down (G minor)

Angie – The Rolling Stones (A minor)

While My Guitar Gently Weeps – The Beatles (A minor)

ACTION STEPS

1. Listen to a song from the previous list and try to play along in the minor key. Pay attention to what notes work and what notes **DO NOT** work when the chords change.

2. Try creating a riff using only the notes from the B minor scale. Not ready to do this yet? Later in the book, after you get through the Rhythm chapter, and the DIY chapter, come back and give this a try again.

10. POST THE TABS!

Tabs are huge today. Everywhere you go online, it seems like people are asking for you to **POST THE TABS!**

Tabs are short for Tablature, which is the visual representation of where the notes are on a particular instrument. All you do is play along to the numbers, and you're playing the correct notes. Somebody else has done all the work of figuring it out, you just follow along, left to right.

Here's an example of a bass tab I created for "Back in Black."

The *letter* is the string — the *number* is the fret.

I've made a few tabs for my YouTube videos. People seem to like them, and I have considered making them for other videos.

Tabs are convenient, and they save you time, but they don't help you learn what's happening on your fretboard. That's one of the main drawbacks for me. Because you don't have to use your ears. You're just counting numbers, and then matching your fingers. It's like a cheat sheet. Which is cool. But I also think it's cool to understand what you're doing.

For the record, I think tabs can be super helpful. I also think you shouldn't get **TOO** used to them. I think you should develop your ears and your hands for learning and hearing notes to become a better overall musician, no matter your skill level.

A SHORT HISTORY OF TABS

Before we get too deep, let's dive into some history. Tabs are old.
Really old. The first known occurrence of Tablature (or Tabs) in
Europe is around 1300 and was first used for notating music for
the organ. Here is a very early tab sheet from Miguel de Fuenllana
from 1554:

I had no idea they were that old! I thought they were invented in
the '60s as a cure for guitarists who couldn't figure out confusing
solos with too many notes. A dedicated guitarist would sit in
his pajamas for a month at home and go through the solo,
painstakingly note by note, and discover exactly what the soloist
did. Then he'd post his findings, and the world would have a
correct research paper (or guitar tab) for exactly how Jimmy Page
played the solo to "Stairway to Heaven."

I've seen a lot of incorrect tabs online. Wrong information on the internet? Has that ever happened before? It has. Don't be shocked. The truth is, people are just doing their best, trying to get it right, and sometimes they (ahem, or we) make mistakes. Out of my 217 videos on YouTube I blew it on one of them. It was the video for "Feel Good, Inc." The first four notes (on the low E string) go 0-0-2-3… and my tab says 0-0-3-5. Yikes! Not even close. Someone brought it to my attention in the comments. They were cool about it, and I made a video acknowledging the error. Because it happens… I should know.

People post all kinds of tabs to their videos, and there's never just one version. Some tabs go full-on crazy and include full music staff composition information. Some are simple, like mine, and only offer the bare bones necessities.

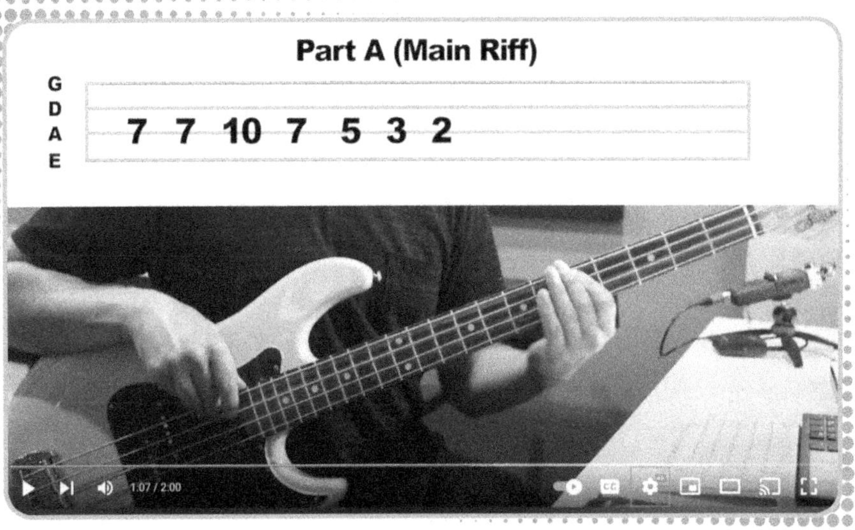

THE MOST BARE-BONES TAB EVER? I DARE YOU TO SHOW ME ONE WITH FEWER.

WHY I DON'T THINK YOU NEED TABS

Having said all that...I don't think you NEED tabs. Again, they're helpful, but just hear me out.

Tabs are a visual and numbers-based system, as opposed to learning via pitch and understanding where the notes are on your bass guitar. That's one of my issues with Tabs. You just know where to go, but you don't know what note you're playing. I'd rather you understand the note you're playing so that you comprehend everything, know what you're doing, and why you're doing it.

If you need to learn something in a hurry, there's nothing better. But if you start to rely on them too much, and you never work on developing your ear, then...

I think they're doing you a disservice.

"But Murphy," you say, "other teachers tell me that tabs are the way to go."

Okay, let's breakdown the arguments FOR them:

A. TIME

You're in a hurry and you want to learn it quick. Alright let's back up a moment. Time? Really? When you fell in love with music and bass guitar, was it to be efficient with your time? No, it wasn't. You fell in love with playing, with music. Time doesn't exist when you play. Why are we in such a hurry? We need to slow down occasionally and remember why we started.

B. YOU DON'T HAVE A GOOD EAR

I didn't either. I had to listen more and put in the time. It just takes practice and repetition to improve your ear. But the difference is, this is music, so the process is fun. This isn't Geometry (For anyone who loves Geometry, I am sorry, but I never liked it and I

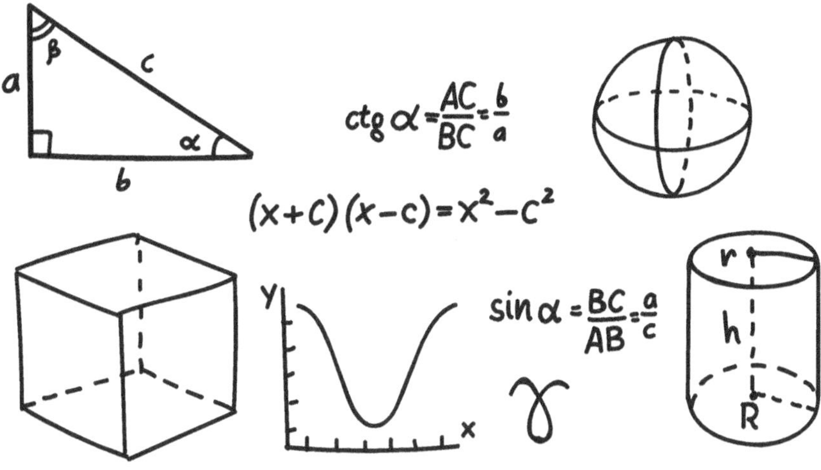

haven't needed it since my last exam in Mr. McNamee's class at Uni High School in 1985). Improving your ear means listening to records and practicing your bass. The more you do it, the better it will become.

Plus, there is more to being a musician than having a fantastic ear. We aren't robots who just need a certain number of cliché things to check off a list. There is feel, groove, timing, attitude, style, instinct, collaboration, promotion, so many different attributes. If you're worried about not having a good ear, I'd argue that some people with perfect pitch *might not be as good as you at some other things*. Maybe they lack in stage presence, rhythm, social skills, songwriting, or something you are gifted at. That's why there are bands. Bands unite musicians of all different styles, tastes, and talents, and blend them into one living and breathing musical organism. We all have different gifts, but the thing that overcomes nearly any struggle: hard work. We can all do that.

C. THEY MAKE IT EASY

All the greatest athletes, CEOs, and world leaders that talk about how they found success, happiness, fulfillment, confidence.... have you ever heard one say that it was because it was easy? No, you haven't.

I know, I know. You might not be trying to become Michael Jordan, Wayne Gretzky, Tiger Woods, Tom Brady, or Lionel Messi. But why not learn a little from them? *Why not?*

For me, taking the TIME, listening to music, developing my EAR, and working HARD has made all the difference.

BASS HACK*

If you think things move too fast online (or people talk too fast) when you're watching bass videos, learning songs... and you keep missing things - I have a trick for you. While you're on YouTube – just click on the gear icon in the lower right-hand part of the video screen. Then choose "Playback Speed." You can slow down the video, or speed it up, and it doesn't change the pitch of the note.

11. THE NUMBERS SYSTEM

I'm pretty sure Marty McFly knew the numbers system when he picked up that guitar at the Enchantment Under The Sea Dance.

Since we just learned about scales which have 7 different notes in them, (8 notes total but one is repeated) I wanted to help you understand the Numbers System. That's when someone says "It's One, Four, Five…" when musicians are about to play a song.

The numbers they're referring to are the numbers in a particular scale. That's it. Here is the A Major scale, again, with the numbers added.

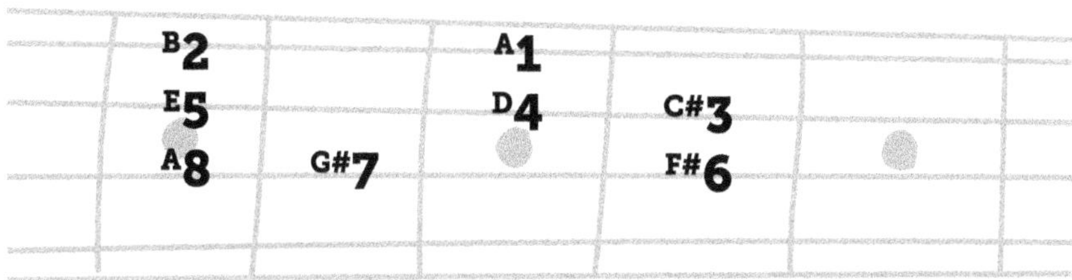

If you're in A Major, and someone says "Just follow me it goes 1–4–5…" Then since you know the A Major scale…
A–B–C#–D–E–F#–G#–A

Just play the number: **1 = A, 4 = D, 5 = E**

The only other thing you'll need to know is how long to go on each number (or note). That depends on the jam, chord progression, or song. You can learn about music patterns and twelve bar blues structure in chapters 18 and 19.

12. WHAT ARE THOSE FUNNY LOOKING THINGS?

Okay, I lied. There are more than 7 notes.

There are 12 notes in music. The first 7 I told you about were the natural notes: A, B, C, D, E, F, G. I didn't get into sharps and flats because you can play hundreds of songs on bass with just natural notes. You don't need to learn Bb or G# to play great songs.

HOWEVER...

There are more notes to learn. I just didn't want to burden you early in the book with notes you won't use too often. But if you want to learn them now, let's do it.

In the graphic below, surrounded by the **ESSENTIAL NOTES** you've already learned, I've marked the places **I HAVEN'T TAUGHT YOU** as Xs. These are where the **SHARPS & FLATS** will go.

But before I show them to you, let me explain a few things.

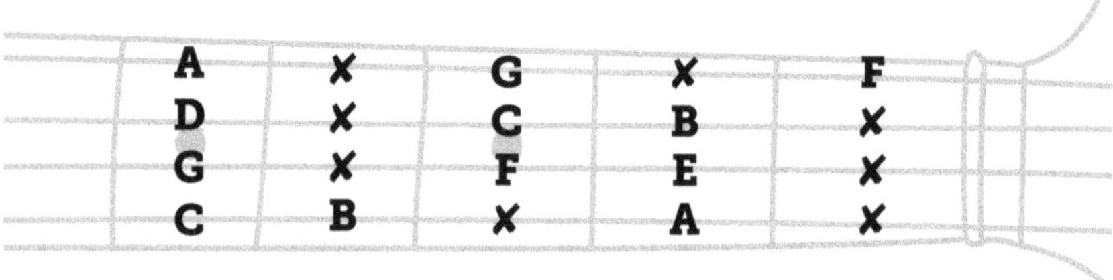

My lie about their only being 7 notes wasn't a total lie. There are only **7 NAMES** of notes, meaning A, B, C, D, E, F, and G. That's it. There is no H, I, J, or K note. Nothing past G exists.

So, if there are only 7 notes, then how do we stretch those 7 to get 12?

Accidentals are the answer!

They're the **FUNNY LOOKING THINGS** we call **SHARPS** and **FLATS** that go next to a note. They look like this:

Sharp: **#** Flat: *b*

If a sharp symbol is next to a note, you raise the note a half step. If a flat symbol is next to a note, you lower it. Pretty simple, right?

NOT SO FAST.

Because it depends on where you are on your fretboard. If you're on C, anywhere on your bass, there is no such thing as C flat, or C*b*. It's just B. Similarly, if you are on F anywhere on your bass, there is no such thing as F flat. It's just E. As you see, we're starting to dip our toe into the abyss of music theory, so I'll just stop there and go back to showing you graphics. Here's where the sharps and flats are.

SHARPS IN THE ESSENTIAL ZONE

A#
D#
G#
C#
F#
A#

FLATS IN THE ESSENTIAL ZONE

B*b*
E*b*
A*b*
D*b*
G*b*
B*b*

If you noticed, the sharps and flats are *in the exact same positions.*

You may also wonder why waste your time calling one single note **TWO DIFFERENT NAMES**.

The answer is because it depends on the key you are in. If you're in a flat key, you use the flat symbol. If you're in a sharp key, then you use the sharp symbol. I don't read music, so I have no idea how to read a music staff with sharps in it, or flats. I just know that that's where they are, so when I need to play a Bb, I know where the Bb is, and I play it.

I've been corrected on my YouTube channel for mixing sharps and flats in teaching a song, which is technically wrong. You don't mix them. But musically, I played the correct note. I just 'called' it the wrong name. See what I mean? It's confusing.

This may be comical and wrong, but the way I remember them is by having favorites. Yes. Totally unrelated to a key, I use certain accidental 'names' all the time, and I don't care if I'm wrong.

Here's how I see **ACCIDENTALS** when I look in my **ESSENTIAL** notes area.

ACCIDENTALS IN THE ESSENTIAL ZONE

That's what I see.

12

I always call the note that sits between G and F as an F#. I never call it Gb. It's just my way. I also never call the note that sits between C and D as Db. I always call it C#. Again, it's just my way. You can take it or leave it.

Here's the deal. If you just learn these Essential Accidentals, you won't be wrong. You'll play the correct sound, in the right position.

The reason I wanted to talk about accidentals is because there are great songs that use them. Songs composed on piano usually have lots of them. "I'm Still Standing" by Elton John has Bb all over it, and some other related notes. I wanted you to understand where they are, and what they do.

Relating to a keyboard, the sharps (#) and flats (*b*) are the black keys on a piano.

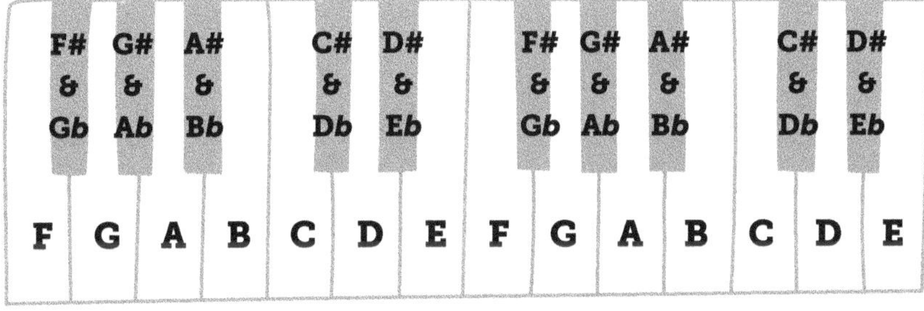

From this view, it's clear why C can't be C flat (Cb). It's just B. And similarly, there is no B#. it's just C.

Same with the E and F notes.

Hey man, I didn't invent the rules, or the piano keyboard layout (regarding why they chose B, C, E and F to sit so close together and have no accidentals between the two). I think it was a guy with a white wig and fancy pants 1,000 years ago. But he was smart, because he invented a great instrument, so let's give it up for him.

Hold the presses. I just Googled him, and I have the answer. I was close. 1,000 was an overinflated guess to be silly, because my first instinct was 500 (so I just doubled it for humor) but I'm stoked because I was S O R T A close. From piano manufacturer Yamaha:

"The piano was invented by Bartolomeo Cristofori (1655-1731) of Italy. Cristofori was unsatisfied by the lack of control that musicians had over the volume of the harpsichord. He is credited for switching out the plucking mechanism with a hammer to create the modern piano in around the year 1700."

Rockstar name. *Bartolomeo Christofori di Francesco.*

Plus, I was close. Wig? Check. Fancy pants? Check.

Alright, back to the bass book. But at least you know when and who invented the piano. Year 1700. And it was Bart, with a wig.

13. HOW TO PLAY BASS

"Keep the cymbals splashy, and let's take the bass line
for a walk..."

Ron Burgundy, *Anchorman*

With four big strings, the role of bass, traditionally, was best suited for
playing single notes, walking lines, roots, fifths, or other notes of
a scale underneath the other instruments. Think of it this way -
while the guitars and keyboards crank out the chords, the bass
cranks out the bottom end to those chords. On a piano, with the full
spectrum of its 88 keys, your left hand is the bass, and your right
hand is the guitar.

While you're responsible for playing the low end, you can also subvert the moment and introduce dynamics and color to a chord depending on what you want to play. Playing a different bottom end to a chord is a **COOL** way to change a chord using **ONE NOTE**.

You have the power to make choices that can add depth, color, and intrigue to ordinary chords. One thing you can do as a bassist is to play a **DIFFERENT ROOT** for a particular chord. Try playing the 5th, 3rd, or the 6th note in the scale, instead of the root, under your guitar player's chords, and see what happens. Krist Novaselic from Nirvana did it in "Lithium" by playing 5th notes under Kurt Cobain's verse chords.

Cobain's verse guitar: E / G# / C# / A / C / D / B / D
Novaselic's verse bass: E / **D#** / C# / A / **G** / **A** / B / D

Krist's 5th notes are in **bold**. When you listen to it, it adds a layer of liveliness to those moments. In the chorus he drops the second note back to the root, G#. If you want to dig into this song deeper, I made a mini-documentary for it on my YouTube channel – search for it and check it.

For THIS BOOK, however, we are going to focus on **BASIC**, and discuss two ways of playing bass:
1. **Play with your fingers or a pick**
2. **Play busy, or play simple**

Both are choices – so let's JUMP IN...

QUESTION #1: PLAY WITH YOUR FINGERS OR A PICK?

FINGERS
The modern electric bass guitar is most often played with your fingers. If you play bass with your fingers, you'll get a warm,

round tone. That's what people most often say, WARM... ROUND. You can tell when you hear it – it has less treble on it when you play with fingers. It's not as "clicky" and it doesn't cut through as much. It's a nice, natural sound for the bass guitar. Slap bass is played with your fingers. The cool thing about playing with your fingers is that there is no interference from anything – just your soft, fleshy fingertips and your bass string. It's always a pure strike – nothing in between.

However, when you're first starting out, it's going to feel a bit awkward. Your hands and fingers won't be used to the big strings, and you'll be sore. It happened to all of us. You're not alone. Just remember, the more you play, the more you'll build callouses, and the easier it will get.

A PICK

Conversely, with a pick, you will get more attack, and a more aggressive tone (although there have been countless bassists who were aggressive with their fingers – Cliff Burton!) It's just that since you're using a piece of plastic to strike your strings, it will naturally be brighter than your fingertips. One of the most common reasons for using a pick is so that bassists can cut through the mix. So that you can hear the bass in the song better.

Try each way. Experiment. There's no wrong or right. A lot of discussions online talk about fingers being the purist way. A lot of the legends did play with their fingers – you can do a Google deep dive and spend hours listening to them – but there are plenty of legends who played with a pick, too.

For me, it was always about the song. What does the song call for? Generally, if it's more laid back, I'm going with fingers. If it's more aggressive, I'll use a pick and cut through.

Play with each and find what's right for you.

QUESTION #2: DO YOU WANT TO BE A SIMPLE BASSIST, OR A BUSY ONE?

I'm aware that talking about playing simple vs busy might be slightly beyond the beginner bass player reading this book, but I mention it because it offers up the idea or dream of where you want to go, and that's important.

There are two factors that will affect your choice to play simple or busy – one is the **SONG** itself, because some songs invite more movement, while others ask for less. The other factor is the **BAND** you wind up in, or more specifically, the **GUITARIST** you play with. What if you looked up and found Eddie Van Halen as your guitarist!? You might be the one laying back a bit.

Imagine if Cliff Williams decided he was going to have busy bass lines all over the place in AC/DC songs. I don't think AC/DC would be as good. I love the way he plays, simple and pounding, so that Angus Young can run around in his schoolboy outfit and play his monster riffs on top. What about Rush? Geddy Lee's creative and intricate bass lines are often the essence of Rush. He's out front with his bass. That's because Alex Lifeson is content to play out

THAT'S CLIFF
IN THE BACK
HOLDING IT
ALL TOGETHER

of the limelight (I had to go there) in their music, letting Lee shine in the open space. It's the same with every band – it will depend on your chemistry and balance with your guitar player.

I WANTED TO BE A SIMPLE BASSIST
Me? I loved playing along with the kick drum and the guitar to form a tight rhythm section because I was a song guy first. I didn't need to play out front. I loved playing hard, attacking riffs that felt like a stiff kick to the chin. To me, that was cool.

Some of those who play simple in their band include:
Michael Anthony, Adam Clayton, Cliff Williams, Tina Weymouth, Bill Wyman, Roger Waters, Eric Avery, Aston Barrett, Colin Greenwood, Krist Novaselic, John Deacon, Kim Deal, Paul Simonon, Simon Gallup, Phil Lynott, Ian Hill, Lemmy, and the list goes on...

On the flip side, bassists who play busier:
James Jamerson, Larry Graham, Stanley Clarke, John Entwistle, Bernard Edwards, Les Claypool, Geddy Lee, Flea, Steve Harris, Jaco Pastorius, Cliff Burton, Marcus Miller, John Paul Jones, Chris Squire, Geezer Butler, Chris Wolstenholme, Bruce Foxton, Bootsy Collins, Andy Rourke, Sting, Jack Bruce, Chuck Rainey, Billy Sheehan, Mark King, Joe Dart, and the list goes on...

***Disclaimer!** The truth is, most of the bassists I put in the 'simple' section could play busier bass lines *if they wanted to*. But in the dynamics of their bands or how they approach playing for the song, they decided to keep it simple. No matter what list you are on, it's **NOT** a barometer for how **GOOD** you are at bass. They're just choices you make.

There are all kinds of different ways to interpret ***how to play bass***. None of them is wrong. It's all up to you.

14. SPEAKING OF INFLUENCES

One of the best ways to find inspiration is to look to our heroes and see how they did it. Remember what David Bowie said, "The only art I'll ever study is stuff that I can steal from."

He wasn't kidding. Your heroes started out just as you are, looking for inspiration, wanting to create something. With Bowie's words in mind, let's look at my heroes on bass.

PAUL McCARTNEY

My first influence was Paul McCartney. Not only because of his fluid and melodic bass playing, which was incredible, but because I think he's the greatest songwriter ever. One of my favorite moments of all time in music is in "Golden Slumbers," where he plays a bass note that is slightly out of tune, and it's set against the most heartbreaking lyric, and for some reason it just stirs a deep and emotional response out of me. To this day I can get overwhelmed listening to it.

"Once there was a way... to get back homeward..."

And then that deep, raw note just pours over me.

I guess it feels like real life – how the note was slightly out of tune, like life can be... and how we're all chasing some form of 'getting back home' to something deep and meaningful in our lives. The fact that the bass note is the thing that draws the emotion out – man, that did it for me. It wasn't an obvious thing – like some rock-star-guitar-god moment, full of fandom and glory. It was a quiet moment, slow and deep, the undercurrent of the emotion, that hooked me. I think most musicians are still chasing The Beatles' songwriting genius through music and sounds.

JOHN PAUL JONES

I know Jimmy Page probably wrote most of the riffs, but the plunging, deep force of Led Zeppelin was John Paul Jones. I got into Led Zeppelin after The Beatles, and I fell in love with their assault of four guys throwing down on heavy riffs. I also loved that Zeppelin were essentially a blues-based riff band that played with monster dynamics. They knew how to play loud, and they knew how to play quiet, and they did it with an astonishing symmetry between all four members. I went on to be the 'riff guy' in a few of my bands, and I can trace most of it back to Zeppelin.

PETE FARNDON

Yes. Pete Farndon. I don't hear many people talk about him when they talk about great bass players, but I loved his playing. His life was cut short, unfortunately, but his talent still shines through so many years later in his fantastic bass lines on the first two Pretenders albums. Check out "Kid," "Precious," "Tattooed Love Boys," and "The Wait." He had a great Fender Precision bass tone that could cut through the songs. This was also the first time I thought, "that dude is the coolest dude I've ever seen." He had a big pompadour of black hair, good looks, leather jacket with a Triumph patch, and just looked like a complete rock star. Great look, killer bass lines.

MIKE ROCHE

Lurching, mysterious, great attacking bass tone, and in a band I loved. Mike Roche loomed large to me when I was a fresh-faced kid in high school. He was the bassist for T.S.O.L., a punk band from Southern California, and I loved his menacing and melodic bass lines. He had a great stance onstage when he played, unpretentious and commanding. He was like the Bill Wyman of punk rock. When I was a teenager, I wanted to be 10% as mysterious and cool as he was, because I felt like the opposite. An awkward teenager trying to figure everything out.

PAUL SIMONON

I've talked about cool bass players, but it's hard to top Paul Simonon. He's high on my list of the coolest and best bassists ever. His creative basslines, his presence onstage, his entire vibe was The Clash, and a big part of why The Clash became known as "the only band that matters." The Clash didn't play distorted power-chord punk rock like The Ramones or The Sex Pistols. Their music had space to it, it had air, and Paul got to weave his basslines through all that open space. Their music incorporated reggae, rockabilly, and pop. His unique and rhythmic basslines are lead melodic parts in some of their songs. If you listen closely, PAUL is often leading the band with his bass, not the guitars, drums, or vocals. Plus, he's featured in one of rock 'n roll's greatest photographs. That's Paul smashing his bass on the cover of their album *"London Calling."*

ERIC AVERY

I became obsessed with Jane's Addiction the moment I heard the opening song, 'Trip Away,' from their debut album in 1987. Perry's vocals and lyrics were the first things that struck me. He was singing about the forgotten, the unloved, the scourge of society and I *loved* it. The other thing that resonated was Eric's basslines. I hadn't ever heard a bassist who anchored every song as much as he did. I also loved that his bass was mixed loud on the records. Jane's songs seemed to be BUILT upon his thundering basslines, and the band played with a fearless dynamic – they could take a song down to the quietest moment, hold it there, and then explode back into the heaviest riff. That aspect of them reminded me of Led Zeppelin. But they also had a punk rock thing going on, with the freedom in how they expressed themselves – I just loved it. My favorite basslines are "Three Days," "Mountain Song," "Pigs in Zen," "Whores," and "Summertime Rolls."

It's always a good time to study the masters and soak in what they do. Eventually you will improve, and you will begin to establish your own style, and then someday YOU might be a musician and bassist somebody ELSE draws inspiration from.

15. UNDERSTANDING YOUR ROLE

For many years on tour, I'd get asked this question over and over. "Do you get jealous of all the attention your singer gets?"

Mark was my singer, and he was featured in a lot of magazines in our time. *Rolling Stone*, *Spin*, and even some mags that weren't about music – *Cosmopolitan*, *Tiger Beat*, etc. A lot of our publicity did happen to be about how good looking he was. He even got some kind of 'Sexiest Rocker Alive' thing – I forget if it was *People Magazine* or what – but when it happened, he commanded a lot of attention. So when we'd get that question, I always just answered with a few stock answers.

"Any press is good press."
"If he's on the cover that probably means you're talking about us... so that's a good thing."
"If it helps get our band and music out there, then I'm happy about it."

I believed my answers, too. I wasn't lying. We were a band. We weren't some put together contraption that might fold just because our singer was on the cover of a magazine. We were a band for seven years before we got our deal. We didn't just come out of nowhere and score it big overnight. We had a longer history than most bands, and we knew it took all of us to do our jobs. We were secure in that. Mark knew it, too. But something about the answers always bugged me. I felt there might be a deeper truth or reason why I was cool with it. Then one day, it hit me. I had my answer for them:

You pick the instrument of your personality.

I don't know how I realized this thought or feeling. No doubt it was summoned partially because of the insistence and regularity of the question, as my mind enjoys toiling over unsolved puzzles. But I'm grateful so many journalists asked me that question because it opened an insight for me as to why people pick certain instruments when they start to play music.

It's how I've answered that question ever since.

15

Because it's the truth. I always thought it was a bit shallow and silly that journalists kept on with that question. What about all the other stuff? Writing, recording, playing? Girls screaming for me? (Yes, girls even scream for bass players in bands on tour, as well as drummers and guitarists and DJs and keyboardists... wait, no they don't for keyboardists). I couldn't have cared less about Mark getting the attention. I'm a bass player. I loved my spot in the back. And I could jump up to the spotlight whenever I wanted, but I could retreat to my spot in the shadows, as well. I loved that. I had my lane. I like being behind the scenes, working on stuff. If I got some attention, great, but it wasn't high on my list of priorities.

I wanted to:
1. Write great songs
2. Be a great live bassist for our shows
3. Keep making a living from it
4. Meet as many girls as possible

The cover of *Teen Beat* wasn't high on my list. I didn't need the attention of a singer or guitarist. I liked slipping under the radar. It's just my personality. Everyone is different.

Bottom line, *I understood my role.*

WHAT'S YOUR ROLE?

Your role isn't just about how good you are on bass. Or how sexy and mysterious you are in press photos. It's about what you bring, overall, to playing and making music with others.

There are all different kinds of bass players. And even though the bass is a simple instrument, there are many ways to approach playing it, and your way will add to the list.

If you look at the icons of bass playing, they all play differently. Every single one brings something to their role. Some are known

as songwriters like John Deacon, Geezer Butler, Sting, the late
Lemmy, Flea, Duff McKagan, Steve Harris, the late Jack Bruce,
and Paul McCartney. Some are also known for their producing
prowess like John Paul Jones and the late Bernard Edwards. Some
are session musicians, like Carol Kaye. Some are just amazing
bassists who are (or were) the glue to their group and that's all they
need to be happy. Some are lead singers like Sting, Roger Waters,
Les Claypool, Lemmy, Mark King, and Gene Simmons.

What is your role? As a bassist, you're supposed to hold down the
bottom end. That's traditionally what you do. But it's up to you.
Understanding your role is an important part of finding your own
voice as a musician.

PHASE TWO: LEARNING MUSIC

16. BECOME A MUSIC FAN FIRST

Music is good for us. Studies have revealed* it can help reduce anxiety, blood pressure, and pain as well as improve sleep, mood, mental alertness, and memory. You can find everybody from Bob Marley, Beethoven, and Friedrich Nietzsche offering their praise of music, and its miraculous ability to do good for us.

Music is not only good for us mentally and physically, it's also good if you're a musician because **understanding great music is where it all begins**. It's where everything starts.

Before you learn to play notes.
Before you learn to be cool onstage.
Before you have style or taste.
Before you develop your rhythm and timing.
Before you master impressive arpeggios, flashy drum solos, and cool pedal effects.

That's why listening is so important.

That's why you have ears.

Listening is our most important communication trait. When a relationship goes sour, it's often because someone isn't listening, while a great listener is often associated with personal success. Talking, on the other hand, is easy. Anybody can talk.

* https://www.hopkinsmedicine.org/health/wellness-and-
  prevention/keep-your-brain-young-with-music

16

As a musician, everything begins with listening to music. In fact, you start doing it even before you know you're going to be a musician. You've been listening your whole life. Your parents might have even played you records in the womb before you were born. I played classical music and The Beatles to my kids through my wife's belly.

Listening to music. Listening to beats, to rhythms, to notes, to melodies, to rest notes, to structure, to non-structure. Listening informs you of *everything*.

Another great thing about listening to music – it's free. Just about anyone has access to music via the radio, CDs, vinyl, cassettes. You can raid the music collections of your parents, your brother, your friends. Hang out in record shops. And for less than 20 bucks a month you can stream almost any song on earth, 24 hours a day, seven days a week.

LISTENING is invaluable.

What happens when you listen to music, is you begin to understand, without even knowing it, the patterns, the beats and the structures of the songs, it all gets embedded in your DNA if you listen to it long enough and early enough.

If you're listening to one kind of music forever, you'll learn that music. But usually, we're exposed to all kinds of music. From friends, family, strangers, radio stations, the internet, YouTube, social media, anywhere. If you listen to reggae, classical, pop, rock, country, metal, EDM, bluegrass, jazz, screamo, polka, singer-songwriter folk, alternative, whatever – it doesn't matter. If you listen to music, you will learn it.

It will become part of you.

That database, that vast array of sounds and rhythms and beats and melodies that grew inside you, from listening, – all that musical nourishment will come out, and you'll draw upon it, and you will make decisions because of it.

But the greatest thing ever? You won't even know you're doing it. People aren't aware that they're playing or writing from their influences.

Sometimes, even the greatest artists are keenly aware they are music fans first.

John Lennon and Paul McCartney did it. They were so impressed by Buddy Holly they:
1. Named their band after his (The Crickets – The Beatles)
2. Wanted to write, sing, and play just like he did. (A rarity at the time – most artists were just singers; they didn't write their own material or play guitar very well. The Beatles were inspired by Holly's to become songwriters and producers, too.)
3. Wore suits like he did (although Brian Epstein is often credited for this).
4. Covered his songs. In fact, their first professional recording, under their former name, the Quarrymen, was Holly's "That'll Be The Day."

ROCK 'N ROLL INSPIRATION!
GLASSES LIKE REG/ELTON
LOOKS TOTALLY LIKE ELVIS COSTELLO
SUIT LIKE THE BEATLES
SINGER/ SONGWRITER LIKE LENNON/ MCCARTNEY

If that's not enough evidence for you to feel alright about copying someone when you're starting out, here's another: a 13-year-old kid name Reginald Kenneth Dwight, who had 20/20 vision, started wearing horn-rimmed glasses just to copy Buddy Holly. Reginald changed his name to Elton John in 1972, and he's been rocking those shades ever since.

Emulate is a more accurate word than copy – because you're doing it from inspiration, admiration, and love, not from a selfish or envious place that would be considered taking or stealing. The good news is that if you do it long enough, your own style will emerge. Your own vision and playing will eventually pour through.

If you keep on creating music, and you attempt to make it your life's work, and find some success, then the COOLEST THING can happen - *you can become an artist that someone else is influenced by.*

A COLLEGE DEGREE FOR FREE

Studying music in a traditional sense – seated in class, with a teacher lecturing and showing examples on a blackboard or PowerPoint – that can be a great way to learn.

But if you'd like to study the best music in the world for relatively no money, with access to all the geniuses of songwriting, composition, structure, harmony, melody, and rhythm in the world, I know a place that has it all. But like any real university, this one has its challenges along with its benefits. Let's explore it:

THE POSITIVES

1. Greatest music ever recorded to study on an endless basis
2. Learn all aspects of composition from the best musicians and entertainers
3. Virtually free
4. Creates discipline and focus
5. No crappy cafeteria food

RAMONES STUDYING HARD AT "ROCK 'N' ROLL HIGH SCHOOL".

THE NEGATIVES

You must be disciplined and organized.

For some reason many musicians or artists have the notion that their art, muse, or talent shouldn't be rushed, herded, or slapped into a militaristic cadence or even organized at all. No one knows why this assumption has carried on, but it has.

You must become a music fan first.

This isn't as simple as it sounds. It's somewhat difficult. What this really means is that you put music first. Number one. It is the most important thing in your life and the thing that you study and dedicate yourself to. Easy to say, not easy to do.

You must grow your ear.

Also easier said than done. You've got to grow your ear because that's how your comprehension of music grows. Don't become stagnant. Stay hungry for learning, for information, for improving.

You must stay patient. The results aren't quick.

This kills it for some people. We live in a selfish generation with a short attention span. Give it to me now. Some people still don't understand the value of patience.

You must do it all alone.
All by yourself. There are, unfortunately, no teachers or guidance counselors. It will take you, and you alone, to achieve this degree.

This incredible university is...

Your record collection. Your streaming playlists. Your music.

So now you see why some of the hardships are there. It's because music is so enjoyable, we often don't consider it a place of intense study. Why ruin it with strenuous listening and scheduling and organizing you may ask?

That answer is up to you.

It all depends on how much you want to improve. Your desires, what are they? Do you want to become better? If your answer is YES, why wait to attend a formal university, pay lots of money, when you can just roll up your sleeves and dig in?

I'm not saying all music study and college sucks, of course not! If you find great instructors who inspire and motivate you to learn, fantastic. Everybody is different, and we all have different ways to reach our goals. But no matter which path you take, remember that many of the greatest artists never had any formal training. They just played with their heart, learned from their heroes, and worked unseen hours to achieve it. The question is, how hard are you willing to work for it?

I don't think you can; **I KNOW** you can. I really do. Because I did it. My parents' record collection and my subsequent record collection

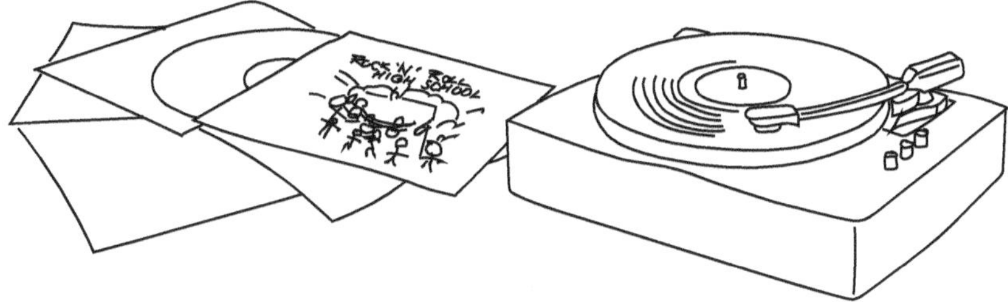

as a teen were my building blocks as a musician. Where else would I have gotten all the stuff that helped me write songs for my band? Songs that ended up on the radio and helped sell millions of albums? Where else would I have generated the melodic choices and chord structures that I could then offer up in song ideas? Was it the hair gel? A friend's good advice? Soccer practice? Pizza? None of the above. It was my record collection. The music. It had become embedded inside me, which helped me make good choices writing and arranging songs years later when we got our deal with Atlantic Records. If you're ready, it's waiting for you. I can't guarantee you'll have the same results I did. But I can guarantee if you dedicate yourself to your music and put in the work, you will put yourself in the best possible position to succeed.

17. HOW DO YOU LISTEN TO MUSIC?

There are more choices than ever for your attention. Social media, YouTube, video games, streaming television, books about how to play the bass. Some of those things are the perfect relief at the end of a stressful day. You can shut your brain off and be entertained by something stupid, funny, interesting, or engaging on a screen. We all do it. But the danger is you can get sucked into learning about fire ants in Brazil as the hours melt away.

You might also have homework, friends, a social life, a girlfriend, a boyfriend, or a job. When you add it up, it's no wonder there is so much stress in our lives and we feel overwhelmed. All those things are fine in moderation, but I wanted to talk to you about how the simple and focused act of listening to music can give you more than all those combined if you pour into it. Especially for you, the musician.

I'm not asking you to change your social calendar. Keep gaming. Go down the rabbit hole on YouTube at 2am occasionally. Don't feel guilty about it. Enjoy that. I just want to help you strike a balance in your calendar with the shut-off-your-brain-video-viewing with something that is also fun to do, but much more beneficial to your brainpower and growth as a musician. All you need to do is add some dedicated **listening time** to your available moments – **not playing music** – just listening, and really focusing your attention on that.

This is how you'll do it...

Find a space where you won't be distracted. Tell your friends you're busy. Turn your cell phone off.

For the music, I want full albums. I don't want playlists. We're going on a journey here. We're going to slow things down, one artist, and one album at a time. *My top records for this exercise are at the end of the chapter.*

I want you to listen to them, doing nothing else, in your comfortable spot. Your favorite chair, couch, floor, bed, hot soak bathtub, whatever, taking it in with high fidelity- or the highest quality reproduction you can get. But not in a sauna. Skip the sauna. Too sweaty.

The idea here isn't new age hogwash. All I'm asking is that you listen to some good music in a way you might enjoy. Where your focus isn't being pulled in 27 different directions.

Your resolve will be tested. You might get asked to do something fun during your distraction-free listening session. You'll have to learn to say NO. Would it be a waste to miss the Friday night party if you stayed in all night and just cranked records and soaked in a night of music? I think you'd survive. There's always another weekend party to go to.

I want you to actively guard your time. It takes work if you want it to count.

Okay, so let's say you've cleared your schedule, and you're ready to dig into some tunes. How?

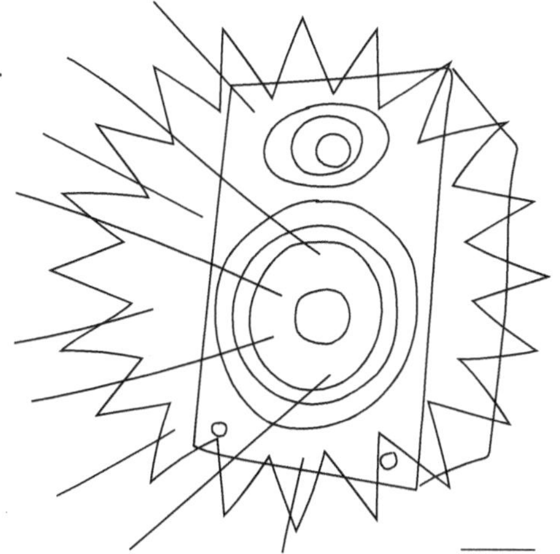

1) Speakers cranked
or
2) Headphone bliss.

Speakers are great because the sound is more ambient, it fills up a room, and it just sounds fat and big. But headphones are good because you're not worried about blasting the neighbors away, and no one even knows you're listening to music.

Headphones are a great way to dial into the true essence of what the producers and artists meant to commit to tape when they made their music. Nothing escapes you when you have headphones on. They send every tiny detail directly into your ears that the band wanted you to hear when they recorded and mixed their record. Headphones drop out the world around you and help you focus.

Listening to music with a pair of good headphones is probably my favorite. My go-to headphones are the Sony MDR 7506. They've been around forever and have stood the test of time and weathered all the trends. They're around 90 bucks. Not too bass heavy, not too trebly. Just perfect. If you're going from ear buds to the 7506, your mind will be blown.

FIND A GOOD LISTENING SPOT

Remember in my intro how I said seven-year-old me loved listening to music by lying on the rug of our living room? That was the spot where my real learning began. In high school, years later, I kept my practice of listening to music by myself. I even got into the curious habit of listening to records in the dark, with all the lights off. I have no idea what prompted me. But you need to try it. An entire album in the dark. Just you and the songwriters with the music between you.

The best memory of me taking the time to listen to music in a unique way was at my friend Miles' house during our sophomore year of high school. Miles had a lot of friends, and I was a shy dork who had his head buried in his music. Miles' mom always let us throw parties, and this one time (probably bolstered by Budweiser),

17

I asked an entire room of partygoers to stop what they were doing and give me two minutes to listen to the beginning of The Damned's "Smash It Up Parts 1 & 2" in the dark. Probably not something that most high school kids would try at a rager. But the music lover in me took over, and I asked them, and they agreed!

So, in 1982, at a party in Irvine full of underage kids who were buzzed or stoned, we all got on the ground and turned out the lights. I put the needle on the beginning, and the record crackle began. On came the warm guitars of Captain Sensible, the fluent bass of Algy Ward, the drums of Rat Scabies. It was a glorious 1:55 seconds. We all just sat there, *listening in the dark. When the fast part kicked in, I threw the lights back on. I had my win.*

Bottom line - find your place where you can listen to music, absorb it, and have your wins. It can be alone or at a party supervised by your friends' mom. Just set aside some time to take it in. It will help your bass playing more than you know.

ACTION STEPS

Listen to an album (your choice) from start to finish, without interruption.

Here are my TOP album choices for you:

1. The Beatles – **Abbey Road / Sgt. Pepper's Lonely Hearts Club Band**
2. Marvin Gaye – **What's Going On**
3. Queen – **A Night at The Opera**
4. Led Zeppelin – **IV**
5. Stevie Wonder – **Songs in The Key of Life**
6. Michael Jackson – **Thriller**

7. The Rolling Stones – **Some Girls**
8. The Sex Pistols – **Never Mind The Bullocks**
9. Red Hot Chili Peppers – **Blood Sugar Sex Magik**
10. The Clash – **London Calling**
11. The Damned – **Machine Gun Etiquette**
12. The Who – **Who's Next**
13. Steely Dan – **Aja**
14. Bob Marley & The Wailers – **Exodus**
15. The Police – **Regatta De Blanc**
16. Rush – **Moving Pictures**
17. Cream – **Wheels Of Fire**
18. Metallica – **Ride The Lightning**
19. Jeff Buckley – **Grace**
20. David Bowie – **The Rise of Fall of Ziggy Stardust and the Spiders from Mars**
21. AC/DC – **Highway to Hell**
22. Nirvana – **Nevermind**
23. Fleetwood Mac – **Rumours**
24. The Beach Boys – **Pet Sounds**
25. Pink Floyd – **Dark Side of the Moon**
26. The Ramones – **Road to Ruin**
27. Black Sabbath – **Paranoid**
28. Pretenders – **Pretenders**
29. Jane's Addiction – **Nothing's Shocking**
30. Chicago – **Chicago Transit Authority**
31. Guns 'N' Roses – **Appetite For Destruction**
32. Joe Jackson – **Look Sharp!**
33. Elton John – **Greatest Hits (1974)**
34. Green Day – **Dookie**
35. Eagles – **Hotel California**

18. MODERN MUSIC HAS A PATTERN

Popular music, going back to the 50s, had a simple structure by design. It wasn't rocket science. Rock 'n' roll was born in this era, and from the beginning, it was made to be simple, catchy, and fun. Early rock was based on the 3-chord structure of 12 bar blues, which meant playing the 1, 4, and 5 chords of a particular key in a looping sequence. It has endured as one of the most popular chord progressions of all time.

There are others.

There's the **U2 PROGRESSION** as I call it, which is based on the chord (or note) sequence of 1-5-6-4. U2 used it for their song "With Or Without You." The song is in D Major, so if you match 1-5-6-4 to a D Major scale you get D, A, Bm, and G. Of course, U2 didn't invent this chord progression, but I think they brought it into the spotlight. The song has almost a billion streams, and it's well known as a bassline that never changes. Four notes for the entire song.

I used the 1-5-6-4 to write the music for our song 'Answer the Phone.' I wrote it in A Major, so our chords are A, E, F#m, D. Play the 1-5-6-4 notes from anywhere on your bass and you'll see why it's a catchy and timeless chord progression.

A couple quick notes: I've mentioned 'chords' a few times. But you're a bass player. This is a bass book! And you don't play chords, right? You're right. I'm just saying chords because it doesn't hurt to know what's playing on top. I like to think of the

BASS ON THE BOTTOM, and **CHORDS ON THE TOP**. When you hear a chord just remember all you have to do is play the root. (We did talk about subverting the moment and adding color by playing something other than the root in the HOW TO PLAY BASS Chapter, true, but pick your moments, as stuff like that is best used sparingly.) You're beginning to see the bass doesn't have to change much to write great songs. "With Or Without You" is nearly five minutes long, and it only needs **FOUR BASS NOTES**. Let that sink in.

Then there are arbitrary chord sequences where you play whatever you want. We're musicians. We make up our own rules.

No matter what chord progression you use, popular songs use these 9 sections:

Think of them as pieces of a puzzle that producers and songwriters use to keep your attention during a song. Since the music doesn't always change underneath these sections, these parts usually differentiate with vocal melodies, catchy guitar parts, keyboards phrases, or rhythm interludes.

Before we examine how artists use them, let's view the **SECTIONS** left to right...

1. INTRO/RIFF > 2. VERSE > 3. PRE-CHORUS > 4. CHORUS > 5. POST-CHORUS > 6. SOLO > 7. BRIDGE > 8. BREAKDOWN > 9. OUTRO

That's better.

We're going to look at 12 iconic songs and see how THEY use the nine sections. I am going to mark down their arrangement, and then after that, check for any patterns. *I'll pull up Spotify and listen along, and jot down what I think is happening. You should do it too – it can help you understand how songs are constructed.*

Chuck Berry / "Johnny B. Goode"	Billie Eilish / "Bad Guy"
INTRO	INTRO
VERSE 1	VERSE 1
CHORUS 1	CHORUS 1
VERSE 2	POST-CHORUS
CHORUS 2	VERSE 2
SOLO	CHORUS 2
VERSE 3	POST-CHORUS X 2
CHORUS 3	OUTRO

Nirvana / "Smells Like Teen Spirit"

INTRO
VERSE 1
PRE-CHORUS
CHORUS 1
POST-CHORUS
VERSE 2
PRE-CHORUS
CHORUS 2
POST-CHORUS
SOLO
VERSE 3
PRE-CHORUS
CHORUS 3
OUTRO

Foo Fighters / "Everlong"

INTRO / RIFF
VERSE 1
RIFF
VERSE 2
PRE-CHORUS
CHORUS 1
RIFF
VERSE 3
PRE-CHORUS
CHORUS 2
BREAKDOWN
PRE-CHORUS
CHORUS 3

AC/DC / "Back in Black"

INTRO
VERSE 1
CHORUS 1
VERSE 2
CHORUS 2
SOLO
CHORUS 3
BRIDGE
CHORUS 4
OUTRO

The Clash / "Rock the Casbah"

INTRO
VERSE 1
CHORUS 1
VERSE 2
CHORUS 2
BRIDGE
CHORUS 3
VERSE 3
CHORUS 4
OUTRO

Buddy Holly / "That'll Be the Day"

INTRO
CHORUS 1
VERSE 1
CHORUS 2
SOLO
CHORUS 3
VERSE 3
CHORUS 4
CHORUS 5

Johnny Cash / "Ring of Fire"

INTRO
VERSE 1
CHORUS 1
RIFF
CHORUS 2
VERSE 2
CHORUS 3
CHORUS 4
OUTRO

Michael Jackson / "Billie Jean"

INTRO
VERSE 1
VERSE 2
PRE-CHORUS
CHORUS 1
VERSE 3
VERSE 4
PRE-CHORUS
CHORUS 2
BRIDGE
CHORUS 3
OUTRO

Ed Sheeran / "Shape of You"

INTRO
VERSE 1
PRE-CHORUS
CHORUS 1
POST-CHORUS
VERSE 2
PRE-CHORUS
CHORUS 2
POST-CHORUS
BREAKDOWN
CHORUS 3
OUTRO

Coldplay / "Yellow"

INTRO / RIFF
VERSE 1
CHORUS 1
RIFF
VERSE 2
CHORUS 2
RIFF
OUTRO

Led Zeppelin / "Immigrant Song"

INTRO / RIFF
VERSE 1
CHORUS 1
RIFF
VERSE 2
CHORUS 2
OUTRO

What is your first impression from these songs? What *patterns* do you notice?

Here are patterns I see: (in order)

1. Start with an **INTRO**
2. Do a **VERSE** and **CHORUS X2** (Mix in a **PRE** or **POST CHORUS** for support)
3. After the second **CHORUS**, do a **BRIDGE**, **SOLO**, or **BREAKDOWN** to alter momentum
4. Do a 3rd **VERSE** and **3RD CHORUS**
5. Tie things up to reach the **END**

Of course, it can vary. Every artist is different. You can re-arrange the **SECTIONS** in different ways, but you'll be blown away by how often this pattern happens. Try it. Pull up your favorite song and mark down the sections you hear.

Two other details I noticed from the 12 arrangements:

1. I noticed that solos are disappearing. Bands don't include them as much anymore. Cue the sad face emoji (Blues and

Jazz still do, of course, as they're built around soloing, and country and hard rock have always kept solos alive).

2. I also noticed Buddy Holly put his chorus first, before the 1st verse, which was very cool and ahead of its time for 1957. The Clash used their chorus as an intro - but didn't sing over it. They just used it as a musical part for the intro, which was clever. My band used the Buddy Holly formula in 1999 for our song "Every Morning," by opening the song with the chorus. We sang it:

"Every Morning there's a halo hangin' from the corner of my girlfriend's four-post bed..."

LET'S BREAK DOWN THE SECTIONS

The **VERSE** and **CHORUS** are the most important sections and are repeated because they do two vital things – they tell you the story (verse) and they get you to sing along (chorus).

If you only have a verse and a chorus, you pretty much have a song. Kurt Cobain even wrote a song called "Verse, Chorus, Verse."

You could have a song with just repeating verses and choruses, but not using the other parts would be a shame. These other parts add dynamics, intrigue, and momentum.

They include:

Intro, Pre-Chorus, Post-Chorus, Bridge, Solo, Breakdown, Outro.

These parts are the supporting cast. They're the flavor creators. They have individual purposes, but together they help set up the verse and chorus to be more powerful than they would be by themselves. Think of these parts as supporting actors from a Hollywood movie. Even movie stars need a supporting cast.

Sometimes they give you a cool INTRO. Other times they introduce a new melody in the PRE-CHORUS or POST-CHORUS. Other times they take the song into a different key or modulation with a BRIDGE to give you a break from the same chords you've been hearing for 2 minutes. Still other times, you want to hear a guitar SOLO so you can air guitar and dream of playing in front of 10,000 people. Then there are moments you want to bring the energy down, very low, to a BREAKDOWN, so the song can breathe before it explodes again. Finally, some songs may need a potpourri of everything at the end for an OUTRO to seal the deal.

LET'S TAKE A DEEPER LOOK AT THE SECTIONS

INTRO

An intro is usually just a verse but without vocals. Clever songwriters often change the music in the Intro to be different from the verse, but most often they are just an opportunity to jam for a moment before the vocals start.

VERSE

The verse is the storyteller part of the song. The singer sings at a lower pitch, moving the story along with clever lyrics and an interesting melody.

PRE-CHORUS

This part specializes in ramping up emotion for the chorus. It helps you tee-up the hook. The pre-chorus is an important tool because it's not easy to go from a quiet verse to a massive chorus in one beat. A good pre-chorus takes care of that.

CHORUS

The chorus is the hook of the song – catchy, memorable, it gets stuck in your head. You want impact here, not story points. A great chorus is often short and staccato to counter the balance of the longer, flowing verse. And since this is the opportunity to push home the main point of your song, the singer usually ramps up an octave or so to add impact.

POST-CHORUS

This helps you come down in intensity from the chorus with a different melody. It doesn't have to be singing. It can be a keyboard or guitar part. The post chorus can often have one of the sneaky-best melodies of the entire song and come back to be overlayed during the outro.

BRIDGE

This is the relief or break from what has been going on for over two minutes with the Verse and Chorus. You get a chance to take a breath-of-fresh-air detour here in chords and melody.

SOLO

Who does solos anymore? LET'S BRING 'EM BACK! Solos were a huge part of music in the '60s and '70s but have since waned. Country is still knocking out solos. Same in Blues, some Rock and Metal, and of course, Jazz. Pop music never really had them.

BREAKDOWN

This happens later in the song when a full reset is needed. It's where you drop the music out and catch your breath. Always comes back in with a big chorus, which in modern language is "The Drop."

OUTRO

An outro is like a huge multi-ingredient soup. You just toss everything in that's lying around - and come up with something delicious. Your broth base is the chorus, mix in some post chorus, a pinch of solo, and a dash of bridge, toss it all into a pot, simmer low, and you've got a tasty outro to end your song well and to give everyone a summary of what they heard.

I hope that after reading this chapter you are starting to understand something about song structure, and you can use it to your benefit in your playing and musical creativity.

I'll break it down even more in Chapter 20, when we learn about how the BASS relates to these different **SECTIONS**, but first... the Blues.

ACTION STEPS

1. Listen to 3 songs and break them down into **SECTIONS**. You can use your computer to do this, or pen and paper, it doesn't matter. Just focus on listening to songs and hearing the different **SECTIONS** change throughout. See how many songs you can do.

19. TWELVE-BAR BLUES

The 12-Bar Blues is one of the most popular chord progressions of all time. Its roots go back to the American South in the 1860's, after the Civil War, born from the agricultural workers who slugged through long days, finding solace and harmony by singing together about their long days and hard lives.

Blues music was influenced by minstrel show music, ragtime, church, and folk music. Its simple form of using the 1 chord, 4 chord and 5 chord over and over, in a pattern of 12 bars, has paved the way for countless bands and hit songs since it began.

W.C. Handy was the first musician to publish songs with the 12-bar chord progression, which took it to a new level of popularity. We all owe a debt of gratitude to W.C., especially since he had to pursue music in secrecy from his parents, who called musical instruments the "Tools of the Devil." We're glad he rebelled against his parents - like a good rock 'n' roller should - to create something that millions of us can enjoy and benefit from.

W.C. Handy, Howlin' Wolf, Robert Johnson, Elmore James, Muddy Waters, Willie Dixon, BB King and others all paved the way for Buddy Holly, Elvis, The Stones, Hendrix, Zeppelin, Aretha Franklin, Chuck Berry, Ray Charles, Little Richard, Albert King, Eric Clapton, The Allman Brothers Band, Stevie Ray Vaughan, and countless others to use the 12-bar sequence.

As an example of the universal appeal of the blues, hit songs have employed its cadence for generations: Billie Eilish uses it today in her hits ("Bad Guy" / 2 billion streams), The Beatles used it in the '60s ("Can't Buy Me Love"), the Ramones used it for punk rock in the '70s ("Blitzkrieg Bop"), and Chuck Berry used it in his '50s classic ("Johnny B. Goode").

The reason why you sometimes hear "12-Bar" and not "12-Bar Blues" is because although it came from the blues, there is room for variation and changing it to whatever you want it to be. It doesn't have to be blues. It's just a great chord structure.

HOW TO PLAY THE 12-BAR PROGRESSION

First let's break down three key elements.

1. **BARS** are the spaces between the lines. That's why there are 12 spaces, or 12 bars.
2. You get **FOUR BEATS** for every bar. In simple language, that's your foot tapping on the ground four times when you're jamming.
3. The bars are divided up by **CHORDS** that relate to the **1**, **4**, and **5** chords of a particular scale (See roman numerals).

Let's try jamming along with this 12-bar sequence. First, pick your tempo. Then pick a key and match the note (for bassists) or chord (for guitarists) of the scale to the roman number in the space. That's it.

12-BAR BLUES CHORD PROGRESSION

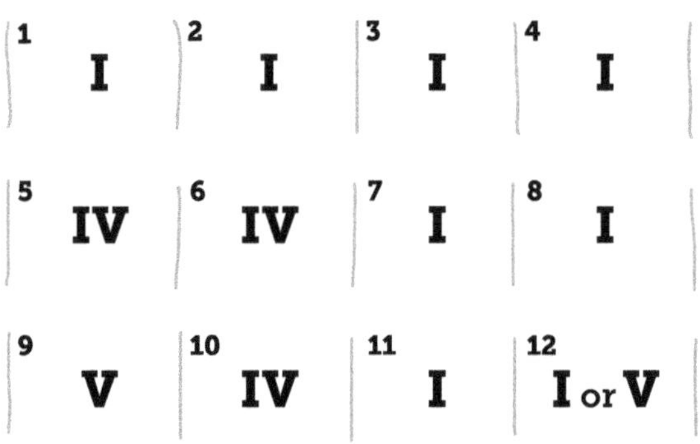

Do you know who this is? He sort of
invented rock and roll, along with
Little Richard and Fats Domino... he
wrote a great song that Marty McFly
played in "Back To The Future," but if
you still don't know... just Google
Keith Richards' favorite guitarist.

Here's the same progression if somebody yelled out, "Let's jam 12-Bar in A!" This is what you'd play.

12-BAR BLUES CHORD PROGRESSION IN 'A'

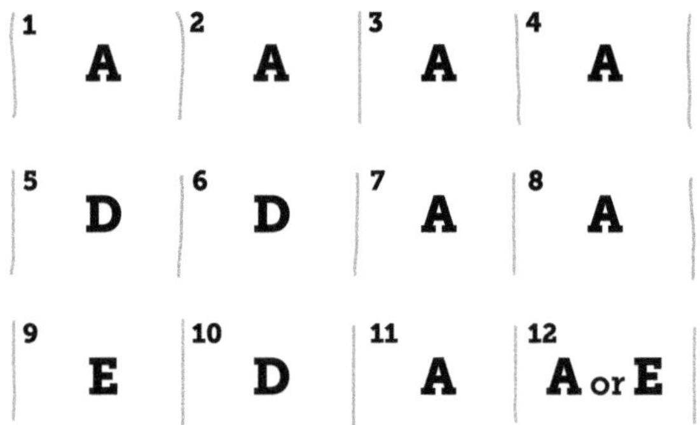

You'd play this because those notes, or chords, match the numbers from the A Major scale. One more time, let's go over the checklist for playing along to the 12-bar progression:

1. Pick a tempo (so you know how fast to go)
2. Pick a key (how about A)
3. Match the note of the A scale to the number in the bars (I just did that for you)
4. Drummer clicks the band in...
5. **ROCKSTARDOM**

THE BLUES SCALE

While we're learning this chord progression, let's learn the **BLUES** scale. It's a fun scale to play.

The note that gives the blues the feel, that sound, is the flatted 5th note, which is Eb. If you didn't get the memo on sharps and flats, jump back to Chapter 12 and check them out.

THE 'A' BLUES SCALE

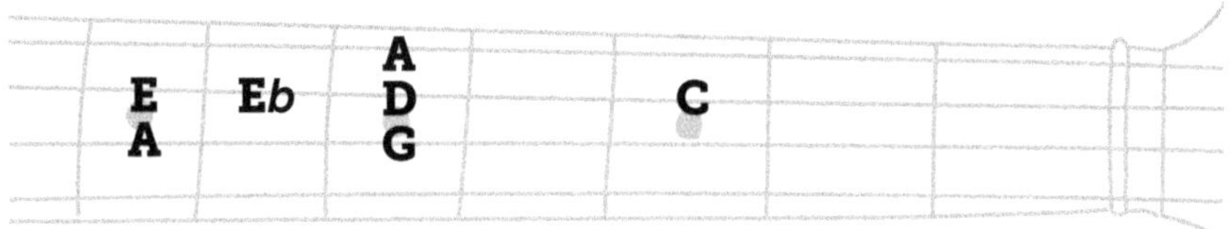

Just copy the shape of this scale somewhere else, and you'll get the same sound in a different key. Here is a G blues scale where the flatted 5th is the D, or Db.

Play these notes on your bass and listen to what it sounds like. Remember, start on the lowest note and play the alphabet. Start on G...Bb...

THE 'G' BLUES SCALE

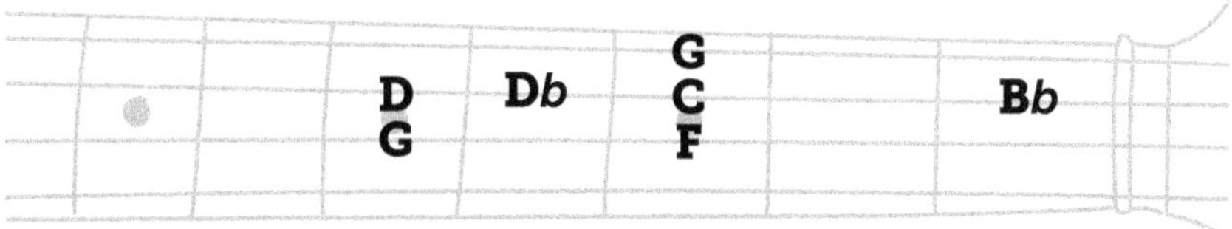

CONFUSING UNNECESSARY IDEAS

Why am I including a chunk of this book called "Confusing Unnecessary Ideas?" Because if you play the bass and do any research, you're going to run into certain theories and notions that won't seem to make sense. I'd rather tell you about them now with the result being to keep it simple, and **DON'T WORRY ABOUT IT**.

For example, if we go a tad deeper and ask the question, "Are the A blues & G blues scales you're showing me Major or minor?" You'd have me there. I think the conventional wisdom is that 90%

of the blues scales you hear are minor scales. This closely resembles the pentatonic minor scale, but I'm going to **STOP RIGHT THERE** because I'm even starting to get confused. The true answer is I don't know.

Let me explain a little further. For this chapter, I was Googling some stuff on blues scales, and I started to get these crazy diagrams that were confusing.

Check them out:

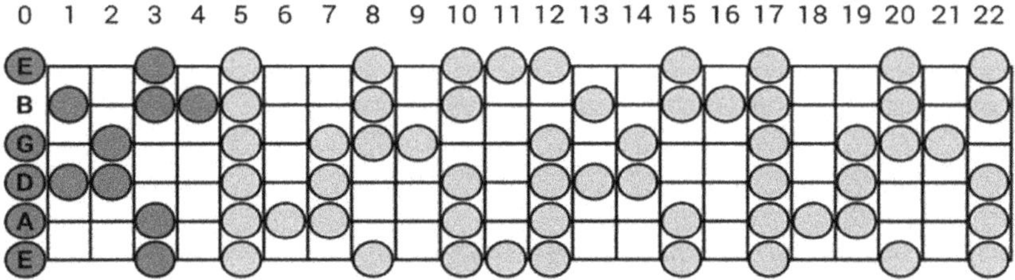

CONFUSING GRAPHIC #1

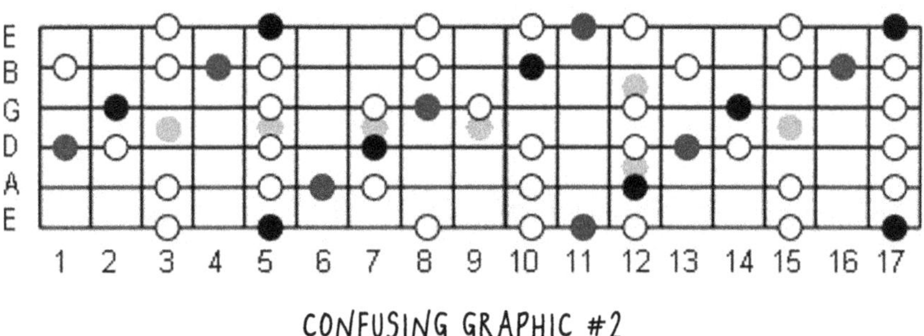

CONFUSING GRAPHIC #2

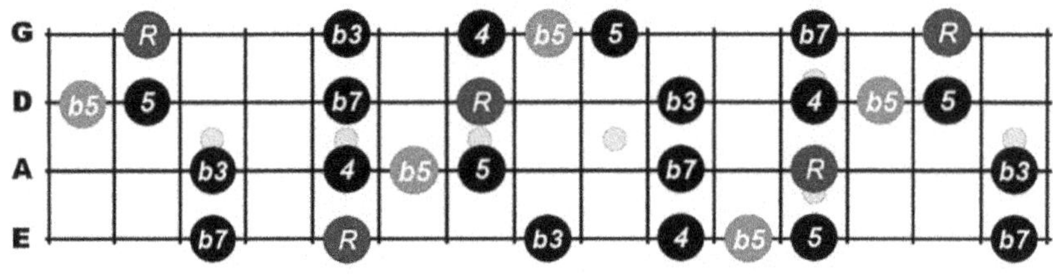

CONFUSING GRAPHIC #3

What the hell *are* these?

I'm sure someone could help me make sense of this, and in fact, in that confusing graphic #3, I can see the root they mean is the 'R' dot, with the b indicating where notes are flat, etc. But why do you need all that on one graphic? Why not keep it simple? Just post a graphic with the minimal number of notes and leave it at that. Do people really want this many notes mapped out for them?

There is good information out there. You just need to search to find what's right for you. Some of you may love those crazy graphics with all those notes. Some of you might loathe graphics and want to learn by ear. To each his own.

All you have to do is go back to those graphics I made for the A blues and G blues. Just play those. Memorize the shapes.

ACTION STEPS

1. Make up your own 12-Bar Blues jam. Try a key other than A since we just did that. Just insert a new sequence of notes based on whatever key you want. Remember to tap your foot with every 1, 2, 3, 4, 1, 2, 3, 4, 1, 2, 3...

2. Listen to:
   Johnny B. Goode by Chuck Berry
   Hound Dog by Elvis Presley
   (We're Gonna) Rock Around the Clock by Bill Haley & His Comets
   That'll Be the Day or **Oh Boy** by Buddy Holly & The Crickets

20. HIT ME WITH YOUR RHYTHM STICK

Rhythm is an important part of learning to play music because when you listen to songs, everybody is playing together, in time, connected and fused through the rhythm. Everybody is jamming together. In *rhythm*.

Ever heard someone say, "I just couldn't get a rhythm going..." and it had nothing to do with music? Like maybe a basketball player who had an off night and couldn't make any shots? Or what about the night he says, "I had a good rhythm... I was getting open and hitting my shots."

Well, that's the idea.

Rhythm is something inside you. It's how you blend into something. It's your strut. It's your cadence. It's your walk, your timing, your movement. The rhythm is the **HOW** of music. It's the **WAY** you play notes.

Some music teachers may start off telling you that rhythm is whole notes, half notes, quarter notes, eighth notes, rest notes, dotted sixteenth notes, triplets, paradiddles, etc. Sure. It can be. Those are note values. We'll get to those. But I want to start big picture. I want you to think of rhythm as two things:

1. Your rhythm when you play alone (your timing, or **how** you play along to a **beat**)
2. The rhythm of a group of people playing together

Rhythm is the thing that adds feel, character, and flavor. I keep using the analogy of food in this book, so here's another – if music is food, then rhythm is the spices, herbs, and hot sauces going into it. Imagine a dinner with ZERO spices, herbs, sauces. It's the stuff that saves your food from being bland.

Starting off with the most basic idea of rhythm, **you need to have good timing**. Having good timing is huge for a bass player. Having good timing means that when you play along to a beat, your playing feels solid. I can't tell you how important that is. Well, I just did. So yeah. It's important. But here's the good news... since you've been listening to music your whole life, you've already been nodding along to beats, tapping your fingers along to your favorite songs, and practicing your rhythm... without even knowing it. What I'm trying to tell you is that you already have rhythm. The trick now is learning to apply that natural ability to your bass.

STARTING OFF BASIC

As I said, I believe everyone has rhythm already inside them.
We just need to build your confidence and unlock your talent for
this wonderful 4-string instrument. The hard part is getting your
fingers used to the feel. It's awkward at first. The strings are big
and not easy to master. That's normal. Your fingers will hurt. I'm
right there with you because that's how I felt. Just keep going and
remember you're not alone – so breathe and smile.

Some practical advice on how to improve your timing:
1. Practice to a drum machine or metronome
2. Play simple (It's harder to play simple – more errors are exposed)
3. Record yourself and listen
4. Repeat

It doesn't matter what you practice. Any kind of bass playing
WITH RHYTHM is good for you.

If the simple essence of rhythm is tapping your fingers on a table,
and the flow of how they play together, then the timing of how
you do it is the foundation of rhythm. Imagine hearing someone
tapping their fingers on a table out of time and all over the place.
It would sound terrible, and it would be annoying. But if that same
person could tap in a cool rhythm, with their timing suddenly as
solid as a ROCK, it will feel different. You would pay attention. **Bad
rhythm makes you tune out, good rhythm keeps you tuned in**.

WHAT I WANT YOU TO LEARN

Regarding rhythm, there are a lot of parameters for notes that you
can use. But I only want you to learn 4:

1. Whole, half, quarter, eight & sixteenth notes (how long you play it)
2. Syncopated (up)
3. Down (down)
4. Rests (silence)

OK... that's 8. But if you learn these 8 things, you can play a lot of rhythms.

Before we start, we need to keep a beat with something. It could be as simple as tapping your foot, it could be a drum machine, or a metronome video on YouTube, or a beat app on your phone. Part of keeping that beat will be deciding how fast it goes. That's your tempo, or the **BEATS PER MINUTE (BPM)**.

Regarding **BPM**, here are some examples:

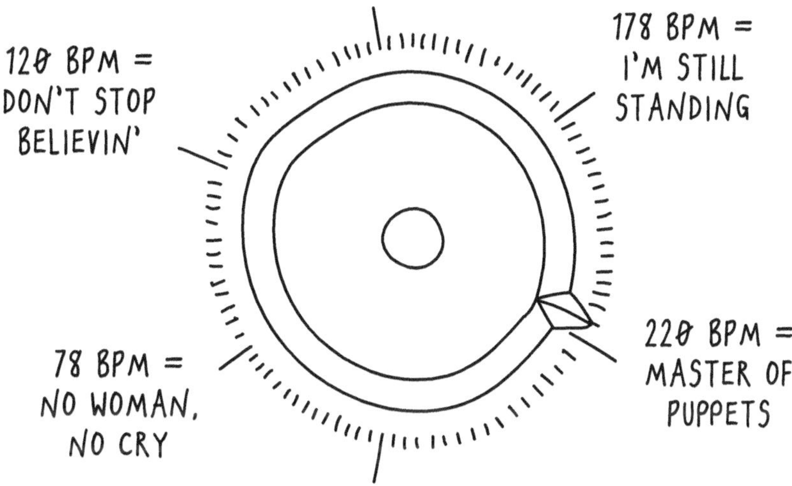

COUNTING THE BEATS

The reason you need to keep a beat is because there is no way to learn about rhythm if you don't have a beat to count it against. You need something doing the **COUNTING**:

One, two, three, four, one, two, three four, one, two....

Whenever you count a number, and tap your foot, that's a **DOWN BEAT**. "One." That's the first down beat, and so on.

Now I want you to learn an **UPBEAT** or a **SYNCOPATED** rhythm. Let's look at counting one more time... but I need to add something to the mix.

One-**and**-two-**and**-three-**and**-four-**and**-one-**and**-two-**and**-three-**and**-four...

If your foot is still correctly tapping on the floor when you say each number, then the **SYNCOPATED BEAT** is every time you say "And." Those are the UPBEATS.

Easy, right? I hope so. (If you don't understand, search for my 'Counting the Beats' video that I made **ESPECIALLY FOR YOU** on my YouTube channel.)

If your *timing* is the heartbeat, or the metronome, then your *rhythm* is what you decide to do along that heartbeat. What notes you'll play against it, or with it. The rhythm lets you make choices.

NOTE VALUES

When you play a note, **depending on how long you let it ring, or how fast you play it against the beat, that equals its NOTE VALUE**. In other words:

If you let a note ring for 4 beats, that = a whole note.
If you let a note ring for 2 beats, that = a half note
If you play a note for 1 beat, that = a quarter note

(The reason I switched to saying 'play' instead of 'ring' is because a quarter note is much shorter than a half note or a whole note. Half notes and whole notes are pretty long. But the quarter note is much quicker, so 'play' sounded more correct.)

If you play a note 8 times in 4 beats = an eight note
If you play a note 16 times in 4 beats = sixteenth notes

ANOTHER WAY TO "SEE" NOTE VALUES

If you can tap your foot and count with every beat, One, two, three, four, one, two, three, four, one, two.... and keep repeating, then here's another way to see it:

WHOLE NOTE = 4 foot taps
HALF NOTE = 2 foot taps
QUARTER NOTE = 1 foot tap

Eighth notes and sixteenth notes get much quicker, so we will describe them differently.

EIGHTH NOTE = Two notes played for every foot tap.

SIXTEENTH NOTE = Four notes played for every foot tap (now you can see why sixteenth notes are called fast!).

If this is confusing to you, do not fear. I have made a custom video, JUST FOR YOU, to explain and **show** this rhythm lesson. Just scan this QR code, and go straight to the video:

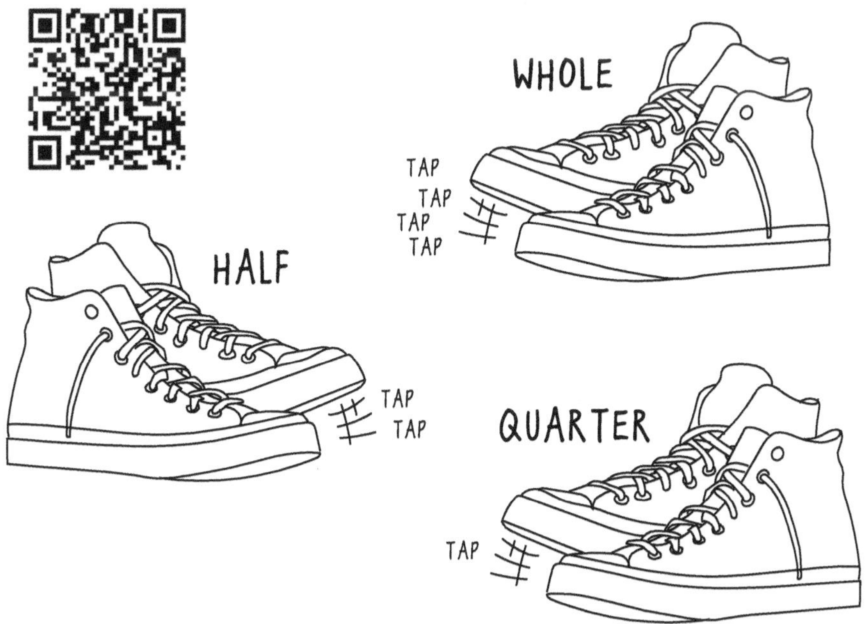

MORE PRACTICE TIPS

As often as you can, you should play simple, or basic, when you practice. This is because more flaws and errors are exposed when you play this way. There is no hiding.

Ever hear a beginner drummer, a few months into playing? They've got that one beat. It's that super-busy, shuffle rock beat. They play that because it sounds impressive and busy. What's ironic is the better they get, the more they'll focus on playing basic, solid drum parts. But I'm no Scrooge – every once in a while, go off, have a blast, play **ANYTHING**. Practice something super hard, even **IMPOSSIBLE**, as Davie504 says in his YouTube videos. Why not? This is supposed to be *fun*.

You should also record yourself. Recording yourself is a game-changer because it gives you accurate feedback of how you sound and play. We often think we sound and play better than we really do. But there's no hiding from a recording. Remember the first time you heard your own voice? Wasn't that a strange phenomenon?

"Wow I sound *funny*..."

Same with your bass. And your rhythm. But instead of hating how you sound – you'll begin to love it.

If you don't have a DAW or a fancy recording system to practice with, just use YouTube. There are tons of high-quality drumbeats out there, all for FREE. I have beats on my channel. Check out the "Drumbeats" playlist on my channel: www.youtube.com/@MurphyKargesBass. For recording yourself just use the Voice Memo on your iPhone. I love mine. It's handy and the quality is unreal. Charlie Puth released an album with vocal melodies and guitar parts that were recorded from his iPhone. That's why his 2018 record is called "Voicenotes."

I NEVER KNEW YOU PLAYED IT THAT WAY

Rodney and I were playing the riff in our song "Caboose" differently for years, and we never knew it. The main riff has these notes: G/C/G/F#/G. It's played AC/DC style, quick, tight, and staccato-ish. As it was written, Rodney syncopates the second note, the C, meaning it goes earlier than the downbeat. But I always played the C on the downbeat. I have no idea why, but that's the way l played it. You'd think someone would have noticed it, that we were doing different things - but nobody said anything.

12 YEARS LATER...

We were screwing around at the soundcheck for the Santa Barbara County Fair, playing old songs, just killing time... when we got around to the song "Caboose." We hadn't played it in years, and it wasn't in our set. So, we started jamming it. I remember, for some reason, I tried to mimic EXCACLY how Rodney played it. With the

Here's Rod and me, waiting in the wings to play a halftime show at the 2001 NBA Finals between the Lakers and Seventy Sixers. It was in Philly, and there was no way anyone would be wearing a Lakers jersey...

C on the upbeat – syncopated. Then he chimed in, and we played it together. With me playing the C in perfect rhythm with him, on the upbeat. But there was only one problem. It sounded *terrible*. Wrong. And it wasn't just because we'd gotten used to playing it that way. It just sounded predictable and uninteresting. A very flat riff suddenly. Then we went back to the way we played it together. With me waiting a millisecond to play it behind him, and it was back! Suddenly, the "Caboose" riff that we knew and loved and had played together for years was back.

It's hard to pinpoint why it was so much better when we were a fraction off from each other, but it just had some cool thing about it. Sometimes, people and their rhythms just gel. Without even knowing it.

ACTION STEPS

Listen to these 25 songs with great rhythm sections:

1. "Cissy Strut" The Meters
2. "Get Up (I Feel Like Being A) Sex Machine" James Brown
3. "Dance to the Music" Sly & The Family Stone
4. "Under The Bridge" Red Hot Chili Peppers
5. "Paranoid" Black Sabbath
6. "Tom Sawyer" Rush
7. "The Real Me" The Who
8. "Good Times" CHIC
9. "Heartbreak Hotel" Elvis Presley
10. "Wait For The Blackout" The Damned
11. "Interstate Love Song" Stone Temple Pilots
12. "Purple Haze" Jimi Hendrix
13. "Jerry Was A Race Car Driver" Primus
14. "Uptown Funk" Mark Ronson & Bruno Mars
15. "Hold On, I'm Coming" Sam & Dave
16. "Roundabout" Yes
17. "Pump It Up" Elvis Costello & The Attractions
18. "2 Minutes To Midnight" Iron Maiden
19. "Walk On The Wild Side" Lou Reed
20. "Ace of Spades" Motorhead
21. "Psycho Killer" Talking Heads
22. "Sober" Tool
23. "Longview" Green Day
24. "Would?" Alice In Chains
25. "Rio" Duran Duran

21. UNDERSTANDING 'KEY'

When people talk about what "key" a song is in, it has to do with the notes of a scale that make up the main part of the song. Usually when a song starts, that's the key the song is in. Let's say you hear a song start in A minor. Then 9 times out of 10, that song will be in A minor.

All you have to do is figure out the A minor scale, and you'll have all the notes (pretty much) that are played in that song. Of course, there are chord changes in every song, but the **KEY** is the relatable set of notes that establishes the vibe, sound and feel from the beginning.

"Hotel California" is in the key of A minor. Let's say a street musician is jamming away to that song, and you want to walk up with a guitar and start jamming with them. It would be good to know **TWO THINGS** prior to walking up:

1. What key it's in
2. How do the chord changes go

It would be boring to hear a song that never changed chords, right? Just strumming away, forever on one chord? Yeah, that would suck. That's why in addition to the KEY to a song, you have chord changes. Chord changes give your song color and flavor. They add to it. But they will always relate to the **KEY**.

ACTION STEPS

1. Find a simple song in G Major without too many chord changes. Try to play along to the song using only notes from the G Major scale.

The Chicago Bulls had just won
another NBA Championship,
and we were playing at The Joint
at the Hard Rock when Dennis
Rodman came over to me to get
down with some SLAP BASS
(I like him even more because
he only wanted to play BASS!).

PHASE THREE: PUTTING IT TOGETHER

22. THE THREE-PART METHOD

The Three-Part Method is my way of seeing music in a simple, broken-down way where you only need to learn three bass parts to be able to play hundreds of songs. Maybe thousands. Sound too good to be true? It's not. And it isn't because us bass players are so thick in the skull that we can only do three parts. Trust me that's not it. Pretty sure.

Before we start, an important clue to the Three-Part Method is that very often, *the bass does not change during different sections in the song*. It's just how the bass operates in popular music. It has to do with how people don't want complicated listening experiences.

Of course, there are variations to everything. Some songs may have more, and some less. But 3 bass parts is a good target to shoot for.

Since you've learned about **SECTIONS**, and how they're used in songs, let's *uncover how those sections are built from a BASS perspective*.

The Nine Sections:

1. INTRO/RIFF > 2. VERSE > 3. PRE-CHORUS >
4. CHORUS > 5. POST-CHORUS > 6. SOLO >
7. BRIDGE > 8. BREAKDOWN > 9. OUTRO

Let's study **Billie Jean** by Michael Jackson. I have broken it down into **SECTIONS** like we learnt in Chapter 18:

Now let's listen to the song and see how many different bass parts exist. When we notice a different part, we'll label them **Part One**, **Part Two**, and **Part Three**.

Just as I did before, I'll listen to the song, and jot down what I hear. You can follow along with me, and we'll discover the bass parts together. Here we go...

MICHAEL JACKSON / BILLIE JEAN

Sections	Bass parts
INTRO	ONE
VERSE 1	ONE
VERSE 2	ONE
PRE-CHORUS	TWO
CHORUS 1	ONE
VERSE 3	ONE
VERSE 4	ONE
PRE-CHORUS	TWO
CHORUS 2	ONE
BRIDGE	ONE
CHORUS 3	ONE
OUTRO	ONE

During the entire song, *the bass only changes once*. Two bass parts for the whole song. Surprising? That's why I keep harping that songs are simple, especially bass parts, and that simple is good. I might even say it again before the book is over.

Let's look at **Billie Jean** one more way, left to right:

INTRO > VERSE > VERSE > PRE-CHORUS >
1   1   1   2

CHORUS > VERSE > VERSE > PRE-CHORUS >
1   1   1   2

CHORUS > BRIDGE > CHORUS > OUTRO
1   1   1   1

Before we figure out what those bass notes are, and get to work playing it, let's look at a few more songs. Here's **Everlong** by Foo Fighters with a note of when the bass part changes.

FOO FIGHTERS / EVERLONG

Sections	Bass parts
INTRO / RIFF	ONE
VERSE 1	ONE
RIFF	ONE
VERSE 2	ONE
PRE-CHORUS	TWO
CHORUS 1	THREE
RIFF	ONE
VERSE 3	ONE
PRE-CHORUS	TWO
CHORUS 2	THREE
BREAKDOWN	NO BASS
PRE-CHORUS	TWO
CHORUS 3	THREE

There are three bass parts to learn **Everlong.** Here's another look at it, left to right: (instead of repeating "One" I just drew a line)

INTRO/RIFF > VERSE > RIFF > VERSE >
1 ————————————————————————————————————>

PRE-CHORUS > CHORUS > RIFF > VERSE >
2   3   1 ————————————————>

PRE-CHORUS > CHORUS > BREAKDOWN > PRE-CHORUS > CHORUS
2   3   NO BASS   2   2

Let's do one more song. Let's do **Bad Guy** by Billie Eilish. Here is the arrangement from Chapter 18. After listening to it, this is how many bass parts I found:

BILLIE EILISH / BAD GUY

Sections	Bass parts
INTRO	ONE
VERSE 1	ONE
CHORUS 1	ONE
POST-CHORUS	ONE
VERSE 2	NO BASS/ONE
CHORUS 2	ONE
POST-CHORUS X 2	ONE
OUTRO	TWO

There's just one bass part in the whole song, with a few stops and a rad little fill at 1:27.

Up to this point, you've learned about the important **NOTES** on your bass, and where they are. You also learned a few scales, what octaves are, and that modern music can follow a **PATTERN** with different **SECTIONS**. Now you've learned the *Three-Part Method*, which is a way of seeing how a song has **THREE BASS PARTS** or less.

ACTION STEPS

1. Grab a piece of paper and pencil. Cue up your favorite songs and start listening to them with the intention of writing down what bass parts you hear.

2. Don't be critical. Enjoy it. Even if you can't get it at first. Remember to slow down, and let the music come to you. You'll get it.

23. LEARNING PART ONE

It's time to start learning a song, without tabs, so let's learn **PART ONE**. I'm going to walk you through learning the **VERSE**.

Don't get discouraged if you can't find the root note right away. I'm happy that you're going to go for it. Stay positive. It's going to be fun.

Final hints before takeoff:

- 9 times out of 10, the root or key will be the first note in the song.
- Don't start playing at first; it might cover up what you're trying to hear.
- First get the root note or key, then get the rest of the verse.
- Verses always loop, and they usually have four notes.
- If it's a moving or walking bass, don't chase it. Let it come to you.
- Use your mouth and hum along like you're singing, to help find the note(s).
- 90% of songs start in E/G/A/C/D.
- Take a deep breath and smile.

FINDING THE ROOT NOTE

Let's start with **"Knockin' on Heaven's Door"** by Bob Dylan. But don't start listening yet. *(Make sure you pull up Bob Dylan's version – that's the one I'll be using).*

Last checkpoint. My left hand is in the **ESSENTIAL NOTES** position. I'm ready to hum the sound of the song as it starts. I'm ready to play one of the 5 notes. I'm calm and focused. Looking for the first note for this **VERSE**.

Okay, let's go for it. Push the space bar and let's start listening. I'll do it with you.

Song begins. Simple strumming pattern.

Let's keep listening...

It sounds to me like there are three (3) notes to the verse. And I know what the first note is. But I want **YOU** to get it on your own.

Keep listening. I want you to get it. *(Don't peek across the page, really try to get it)*.

If you don't have it yet, remember don't play your bass too often, it might cover up what you're trying to hear. Make sure your bass isn't turned up too loud, just enough to blend into what you're listening to, but a fraction louder so that you can hear if what you're playing is right.

Okay going to tell you what the first **NOTE** is....

It's **G**.

G is the first note. And the song is in G Major. Got the second note? Maybe you're doing great, and you already have it. If you don't, I'll give you another second.

Okay, ready? *(If not, don't peek below, keep going - you'll find it!)*

The second note is...

It's **D**.

So, we've got the **VERSE** at G, and D.

We're looking for the third note in the **VERSE**. Here's where it gets a little tricky. Bob Dylan wrote this song, and for the third note he alternates between two different notes. I figured it out. Did you?

Okay... the first time the song starts, he plays....

G, D, then **A**.

But the next time through he plays...

G, D, then **C**.

This is how the song goes the entire time. **G, D, A** then **G, D, C**.... and you repeat it until the end.

So, it's:

VERSE   CHORUS

G, D, A – G, D, C   G, D, A – G, D, C

The song is just a verse and a chorus. Nothing else. No filler. Great, classic song. Guns N' Roses did a well-known cover of this song on their *Use Your Illusion II* record. But when you listen to their version next, it'll sound funny, it'll sound out of tune. That's because they, like we did in Sugar Ray, tuned their guitars and basses down a ½ step. People do this so their songs and music sound a bit lower and heavier, and it also helps singers hit the high notes.

MORE ON HALF-STEP DOWN TUNING

It's an old trick that has been going on since the '60s with mostly guitar dominant bands doing it – some who have done it are: Jimi Hendrix, Black Sabbath, AC/DC, Van Halen, Kiss, Stevie Ray Vaughan, Nirvana, Metallica, Alice in Chains, Jane's Addiction, Smashing Pumpkins, and others.

Half-Step Down Tuning happened a lot in the '90s too, but it's less popular now because there are fewer guitar heavy bands around. Looking back, it makes it kind of a pain in the arse because people think our song "Fly" was written in Ab, "Mean Machine" was written in Db, etc. They were *technically*, but we didn't play them in those positions on our guitars. We played "Fly" in the position of A on our basses and guitars, and we played "Mean Machine" in the position of D. We reasoned that if it was good enough for Eddie Van Halen, it was good enough for us.

If you followed along and did your best, great job. The point isn't if you got it right or not. The point is, you tried to learn something with your brains, your ear, and your hands. *Without* tabs. If you got some or all of it right, then good on you, congrats. Let's keep going, and keep playing and learning, and having fun at it.

Let's roll into the next part, **PART TWO**.

24. LEARNING PART TWO

Since "Knockin' on Heaven's Door" has just one part, we can't use it to learn a second part. Let's find a song that has 3 parts, and I'll walk you through learning **PART TWO**, which will be the **CHORUS**.

The last chapter was all about learning the first note from the start, then figuring out the rest of the verse. When you figure out what the verse is, sometimes that can give you a clue to the chorus. There are just certain notes that work when you're moving from here to there in a song.

"Have You Ever Seen the Rain?" by Creedence Clearwater Revival has a brilliant, fantastic melody. Pull the track up on your favorite streaming device, record player, 8-track cassette, CD player, or mp3 player, and push play on the top of the song. Let's listen down to the end of the song and get an idea of the feel of it, so we can get ourselves ready for the change after the verse.

Actually, HOLD ON - I changed my mind. I want you to figure out the first note and verse of this song, too. Even though this chapter is focused on you learning **PART TWO**, this just gives us more practice. Let's jump into it.

Okay, I'm listening now...

Great song. This is a masterclass in songwriting. John Fogerty, the singer and main songwriter, uses an intro that isn't just the verse. When the bass and vocals kick in, that's the verse. That's what we'll be focused on learning first.

No tabs. Just your ear, your bass, and your talent. I know you can do this.

I'll give you a hint. The verse is only two notes. Keep listening and do all the tricks I mentioned to help you get the notes. *(Hands in essential positions. Be patient. Hum along and try to match the sound with your bass. Don't chase it.)* Did you get it? The first note?

Okay here it is...

It's **C**.

This song is in **C Major**. My "90% of all songs start in E/G/A/C/D" is still alive! Did you get the second note in the verse?

The second note is...

G.

So, the verse is:

C, **G**.

"Have You Ever Seen the Rain?" goes like this for the verse:

1	C	2	C	3	C	4	C
	////		////		////		////

5	G	6	G	7	C	8	C
	////		////		////		////

Just count the marks in between the grey bar lines as "1, 2, 3, 4". Each mark represents a note. Repeat for each new bar, playing each of the notes. Easy.

24

Now you're playing along with the music, following the notes, counting the time, AWESOME! So that's the verse, and now that we're here to learn **PART TWO**, let's finally get on with it. Go ahead and listen to the **CHORUS**...

The first couple notes of the chorus aren't too hard. The second part does a walkdown line that may be hard for some of you to pick up. My advice, just get the very first part before you worry about that walkdown part.

The chorus notes for the bass go like this...

F, **G**.

Then the walkdown...

C, **B**, **A**, **G**... (then back to the **F** and **G**).

So, the chorus is:

F, G, C, B, A, G

So, for the bars breakdown, it would look like this (grey notes are the walkdown – they move quicker):

1 **F** / / / /	2 **G** / / / /	3 C B / / / /	4 A G / / / /
5 **F** / / / /	6 **G** / / / /	7 C B / / / /	8 A G / / / /
9 **F** / / / /	10 **G** / / / /	11 **C** / / / /	12 **C** / / / /

There is another walkdown lick that is done in the intro and at the
end of the chorus that I didn't put in the diagram above. You don't
need to learn that right now because playing C is just fine, and
sometimes when you play licks, you still need a root chord
underneath. C is it. So you're good. If you can figure out that lick,
bonus points for you. Great job if you got through this verse and
chorus with me.

LEARNING PART THREE

At one point in the writing of this book, I had a "Learning Part
Three" chapter that came next. Obviously, right? Three-Part Method!
But since the last two chapters have covered everything you need
to know about the process of learning new bass parts, you can just
repeat the process no matter how many parts a song has.

25. BREAKING DOWN A SONG IN SECONDS

I want to show you how you can break down a song in seconds, putting the Three-Part Method on paper, creating my version of "Sheet Music."

This is helpful for two reasons, one, it helps you learn how to breakdown songs by sections and notes, and two, it creates something real and tangible that we can use to follow along to songs we haven't memorized yet.

Grab a Sharpie, some paper, and cue the song up however you listen to music. All you have to do is listen for sections of the song where it makes changes. Here we go...

'SMOKE ON THE WATER'

The beginning of the song has that classic guitar riff, then all the other instruments fall into place. This is the **INTRO**. Write that down in big, blocky letters and give it a (1).

The verse, if you've been following the book, is the story part of the song. The singer will begin telling the story to draw you in. This is the **VERSE**. Write that down as well. The bass changes, so we'll give it a (2).

"Smoke... on the water.... A Fire in the sky..." goes the **CHORUS**. Write that down. Give it a (3) because the bass changes again for the chorus.

Here's what the drawing will look like:

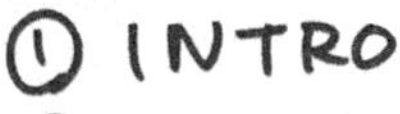

Don't worry about figuring out the bass notes just yet. You're just mapping out what the song does big picture. Let's keep going. If you map out the rest, it goes like this:

That's what the song looks like on paper... in STRUCTURE and in BASS PARTS. If you knew the notes of those (3) parts, you could go out and play it right now. *I wrote the solo as a 4th part, but in truth it's just the verse played a little bit different. There is also a cool little fill at the end of the solo, but that's just something you'll learn as you move along. I wanted to acknowledge it being a bit different,, but it's still primarily 3 parts.*

25

The next step is to learn the notes. Since you know where your **ESSENTIAL** and **YES** notes are, you can find the notes 2 ways:

1. Figure them out using the lessons in chapters 23 & 24.
2. Watch someone play it in a video and use your knowledge of the notes on your fretboard.

There are more professional and impressive ways people do this, but this is **MY WAY**.

All I need the sheet to do is show me where I am (**SECTIONS**), and remind me what to play when I'm there (**NOTES**). Here's what the structure looks like with the NOTES filled in:

As you can see, there is some shorthand going on. Little bits and pieces of information to help us navigate the song.

① INTRO (G,C,Bb)
② VERSE (G,F) SIMPLIFIED!
③ CHORUS (C, Ab, G. then Riff)

① INTRO
② VERSE   ''
③ CHORUS
① INTRO   (G,C, Bb)
④ SOLO   (vary on intro - Riff in G

① INTRO
② VERSE   ''
③ CHORUS

① INTRO (to fade) (G,C,Bb)

The root notes of the verse are simple. It's just G and F. But Roger Glover absolutely crushes it by playing a really cool and complex bassline during the verse and solo.

Although he's busy in those sections, and playing a lot of notes, he's pretty much just playing notes from a G minor scale, based on the chord progression in the song.

So, if you wanted to follow along, and keep it simple, you wouldn't be wrong to just play the root notes, G and F, until you figured out the more difficult part he's doing later on.

Since you were warned of my simpleminded approach, I'm relieved of the shame this whole process may seem to someone who is refined in the art of professional sheet music. If sheet music is like a five-course meal, mine is a slice of pizza and a Coke. They both get the job done. Mine just has a little more grease.

If you think this may work for you, and you like my messy handwriting, then I'm stoked for you. I think you may come to enjoy having a song sheet created this way, in *your own* writing, that will help you remember what you need to know to play something, and also continue to help you understand how songs are built and constructed.

Bottom line, cram in whatever notes you need in addition to the SECTIONS, and the NOTES, which help keep you knowing where you are in the song, and what note to play there, respectively.

NOW GO AND LEARN ONE ON YOUR OWN

You're ready to double down on your confidence and attempt to learn a song on your own. With only your ears. No tabs. Not outside help. Just get a pen and some paper and start having fun mapping out songs. Then find the notes for the 3 parts... and you're on your way.

ACTION STEPS

1. Do three songs like this. Choose simple songs. Easy ones. Use a Sharpie, and some clean paper, and write out their structures and their bass parts. After you've structured it like this, then try to use your ear to figure out the notes. Don't give up and use tabs! I know you can do it. At LEAST try to get ONE SONG done without tabs.

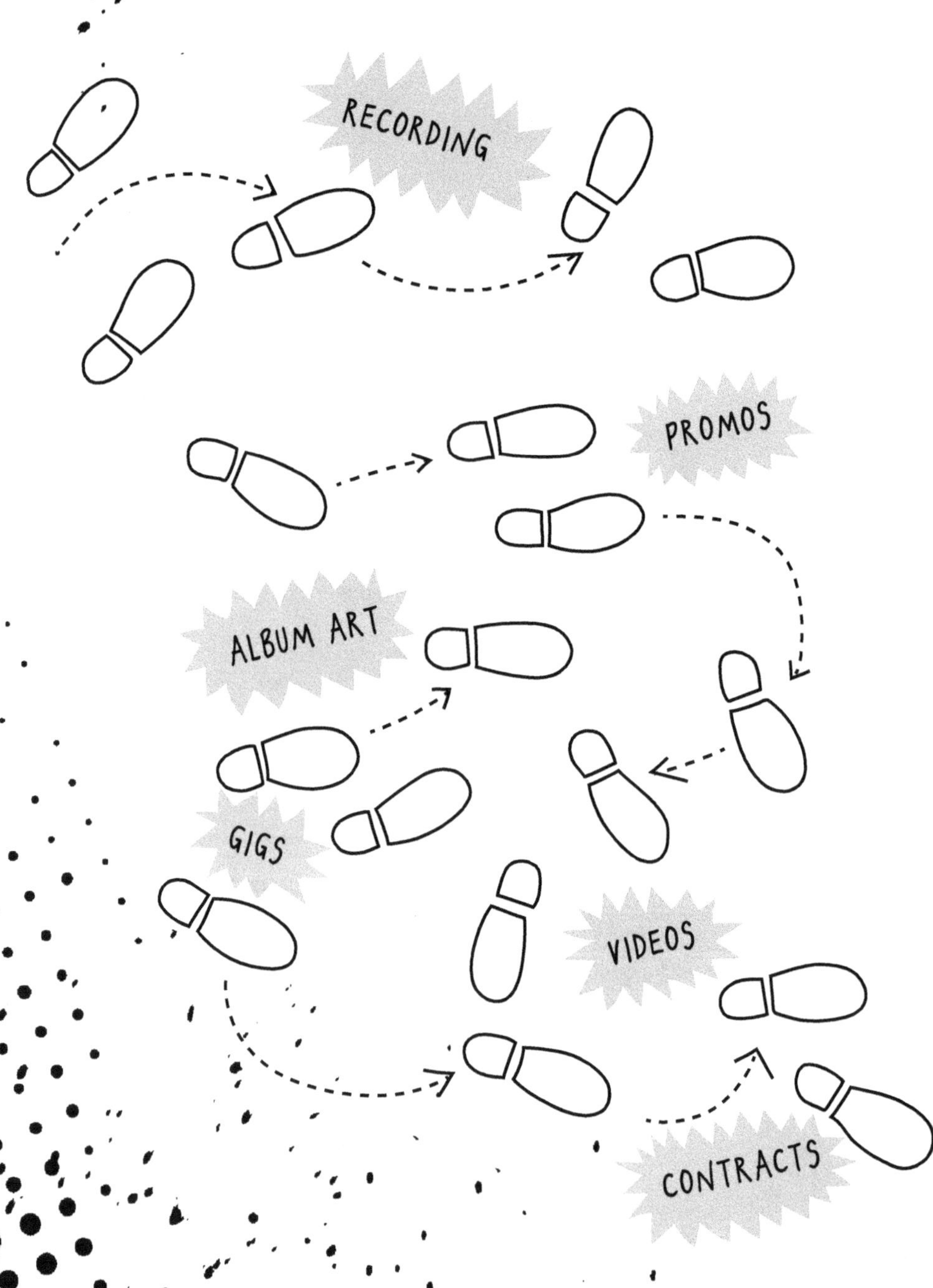

RECORDING
PROMOS
ALBUM ART
GIGS
VIDEOS
CONTRACTS

PHASE FOUR:
NEXT STEPS

26. MEETING PEOPLE

Now that you've learned the basics about playing the bass, I thought it might be helpful to also learn what to do next.

Music is the key, and it's what we all love to play and do. But at every phase you need other people to help you, no matter what level you are at, to do your thing with music. No matter if you are a just a beginner banging away in the garage, or if you're a professional musician touring and selling out venues – it's all about people. I knew we needed people around when Sugar Ray was doing their thing, but I never fully understood it to the degree that I do now.

DOUG MORRIS, THE OLD SCHOOL LABEL BOSS WHO SIGNED A GARAGE BAND FROM NEWPORT BEACH TO A 2.1-MILLION-DOLLAR DEAL IN 1994. WHAT'S THAT PRORATED FOR TODAY? THANKS DOUG!

You can have great music, you can play well, but the people you choose to put around you are the determining factors to how well you will do – on any level.

You may write songs alone, but you don't record alone. You don't put your music out alone. And even if you release a song like Billie Eilish's "Ocean Eyes" that you recorded on a laptop in your bedroom, you will also be approached by "label people" who want to sign you and want to collaborate with you.

You also need help...

RECORDING YOUR MUSIC

PUTTING ON LIVE SHOWS

ORGANIZING AND OPTIMIZING SOCIAL MEDIA

TAKING PHOTOS IN THE STUDIO & ON THE ROAD

SELLING MERCHANDISE AT LIVE VENUES

FILMING & EDITING MUSIC VIDEOS

DESIGNING ARTWORK

What about promoting your band? Traditional radio is still there, so are influential blogs, and streaming playlists. If you become successful, you'll be spending a lot of time meeting and working with all these people. The point of understanding all this is that these people love their work just as much as you love making music. They should all be treated with the same respect that you should be treated with when people work with you. You are ALL in it together.

I would be writing a different book if I hadn't found Craig, Mark, Rod and Stan. I was lucky to find four different and talented guys to collaborate with. I don't know why things come together in some situations and why things fall apart in others.

THE UK TOUR GUY
THE TECH GUY
THE VIDEO GUY
THE STUDIO GUY
HIS BOSS
THE GUY HE KNEW AT ATLANTIC
THAT GUY'S FRIEND ON TOUR
THE GUY WITH THE VAN
DAD'S FRIEND
MY DAD
THE BAND

If you keep going and stay positive - it will pay off for you. Don't lose faith. It's not easy. But it's all worth it in the end – when you're standing on a stage somewhere, the crowd is hushed and listening to your music... and all the hours you spent working to get there feel better than you ever imagined.

IT TAKES MORE THAN YOUR BANDMATES TO BE SUCCESSFUL

Life is more interesting than we know. Strange things happen, and someone who you never imagined might give you an assist in your pursuit of music. My father, of all people, got us the connection to get our managers, who subsequently got us a record deal with Atlantic Records. Who knows what would have happened if my father never introduced us to Randy Heiman?

How would our path have been different? Would the song "Fly" even exist?

After we were on Atlantic Records, they helped us meet our producer, David Kahne, who was a big part of our success. I could go on and on about how the people who you surround yourself with are just as important as all the hard work. If you wind up with bad people, you have no chance. But good people, you have a shot. That's all you want. A shot.

You want to align yourself with people who believe in you. Even if you're wrong, or possibly delusional about your goals, you need friends to help push you through those doors. They'll pump you up, give you that fire when you're running low. You can't do it alone. No matter how hard you try.

The right people will improve your life and grow your chances of success.

But for you, right now, the beginning bassist, even if you're light years away in your mind from a record deal, the principle still applies that you must be able to deal with people well. You need to communicate clearly with those around you, no matter your skill level. If you're a crappy communicator when you're starting out, you'll be a crappy communicator when you're at the top of the charts and cruising around town in your Porsche. In fact, you'll probably be crappier. So, let's take a look at those around you now...

PEOPLE ARE THE KEY

Your parents. Because you're living with them, they're paying the mortgage or rent. So you live by their rules. Understand this, and respect it. Be clear with them in your desires and choices. Don't hide anything, and don't be ashamed of what you like. If they don't agree with you, that's their prerogative, and they're entitled to it because they're paying the bills. When you eventually move out and create your own life, you can do whatever you want. For now, respect them and work hard so your future can be bright.

Your friends. Your friends are a huge part of your life. They're who you spend most of your time with. Choose them wisely. I like Henry Ford's quote – "My best friend is the one who brings out the best in me." Take his wisdom to heart.

Music teacher. Big one. As you have heard in this book, my experiences with lessons were not great. Thankfully, there are great new options to learn and get inspired by music. The School of Rock is a solid choice. There are other regional rock schools you can get connected to as well. Utilize these places and connect with peers, find inspiration from instructors, and start jamming in a band.

Recording studio. Yes. YOU. Even if you're just a beginner bassist, you can learn enough to do a simple recording. Why not? I say YOU CAN. For this you can either just download some software and do it yourself on a computer, or have a friend do it for you. OR you can go to a real recording studio and have an engineer do it for you. It's extremely fun and mind blowing the first time you walk into a recording session. The moment you enter, from the first time you hit record, to the last mix of the demo, you can't believe you're there and doing it. Be cool to everyone you meet at the studio. You'll never know where or when you'll see them again.

Other musicians. If you're a beginner or intermediate bassist, you need a band, right? Learning alone is ok, but playing with others is where it's at. That's why bands are so cool. That's why it's so much fun. The BAND. It's like a gang. Okay, not really, but go with it. You have people who believe as you do, who want to support you, who have your back, and who you will be growing close with because you'll be doing music together. Making music creates a bond. These musicians can come from anywhere. Friends, enemies, strangers. The key is to keep an open mind. You never know where it will lead.

Local clubs, coffee shops, gigs. You've gotta play somewhere. If you get into a band, and you get a setlist together, and you feel you're ready, then get out there and give it a shot. You'll need other people to believe you are good enough to play at their place, so do your part, work your tail off, and crush it onstage when you get the chance.

WHAT YOU BRING TO THE TABLE

It's important to understand what you bring to the table. You don't just bring yourself, your physical body, standing there. You bring your habits, your personality, your quirkiness, your effort, your baggage. You bring everything. So do the other musicians.

I like to think of all this stuff we bring to the table as huge sacks of invisible baggage that we drag behind us. And perhaps "baggage" is too negative a word. Let's call it stuff. Because stuff can be good – it could be anything – your truck, your listening skills, your resources, your money, your looks, your talent, your motivation, your humor.

DON'T FORGET TO LOOK AROUND

Even though you must put your head down and work hard, don't keep your head down for so long that you miss everyone passing by. As dedicated as you may be, remember that you don't play music to wind up in your room in your underwear in front of a mirror. You play music so you can one day perform in a theater packed full of fans, who are mesmerized by the songs you're playing with your band.

Because if you do have success someday, your life will get busy. You'll be shuttled around playing in different cities. Your days will be stacked full of interviews, radio visits, meetings, soundchecks, gigs, after parties, co-writes, tour buses, airports, train stations, midnight truck stops, hotel parties, and meeting so many new people your head will spin. It will get exhausting sometimes and you'll want to withdraw into a space of your own where you can find *you* again. Always take that time to re-charge, but never forget that this journey is about people, so as soon as you can, get back out there, shake hands, and bring it all on with a wink and a nod to the fact that it might only be this good for so long.

Enjoy the ride and smile.

27. CONFIDENCE

Let me ask you a question. Are you confident in anything? Is there one thing you can do very well? Doesn't matter what it is. I'm talking about *anything*. I bet there is. And when you think about it, I bet it makes you feel good.

That's because you're competent at it. You're good at it. Maybe an expert. I don't exactly know why it makes us feel good when we're adept at something. But it does. It fills us with **CONFIDENCE**.

I'm not just talking about the obvious things: strength, intelligence, speed – those are great. I'm talking about the ability to judge the flavor of your coffee, if your creamer is 2% or whole milk, or if there is an artificial sweetener in your soda (I can't stand artificial sweeteners – just gimme the sugar). I'm talking any skills – the ability to judge someone or read people, park cars, or make people laugh. Perhaps it's a strange skill you have around your home, like you're the only one who can fix something – a leaky faucet or a jammed door that doesn't open well. Maybe you're the best at hitting an open shot into the wastebasket with a wadded-up piece of paper. I'm just talking about anything that you, somehow, have become **THE BEST** at handling.

If you're someone who doesn't think they're an expert at something, anything, then you're WRONG. I know you are. Let me prove it to you.

EVERYONE IS TALENTED, ORIGINAL, AND HAS SOMETHING IMPORTANT TO SAY

One of my favorite books is *If You Want to Write* by Brenda Ueland. It came out in 1938. Brenda published over 6 million words in her lifetime. She wrote that everyone is "talented, original, and has something important to say." I was like, "Wow. Really?" Is she just saying that to be optimistic, or can it be proven? If you check out her book you'll be blown away as she proves it to be true by referring to scientific data, common sense, logic, and some other conclusions from the human condition that will leave you inspired and optimistic.

My takeaway from her book as it relates to **YOU BECOMING REALLY GOOD AT PLAYING THE BASS** comes down to one thing:

YOU MUST BELIEVE YOU CAN DO IT.

It's not a little thought. It's asking you to be bold. It's asking you to be brave and shake off the negative influences in your life when they come in to raid your dreams and tear you down.

You're reading this in a book *right now*, but when they come to you in person and start ripping you apart for what you're trying to achieve, just remember that history is filled with stories of people who were misunderstood and underappreciated who went on to greatness.

Greatness.

Let it fire you up. Let it inspire you. Keep it with you – not as a negative thought to burden – but as a little ball of potent determination. Use it for when you want to show people how wrong they were because you love music more than anyone could know. And you will prove it to them by being successful someday – and perhaps years from now they will buy a ticket to a concert and – completely unaware – they will sit down with their overpriced beer and lame date and realize when they look up from their seats in the 34th row that they are watching *you* play in the band, and everyone is screaming and cheering for *you*. And then of course that same person will try to find you to get backstage

This is me about to play "Fly" for the 100th time. At this point I could play it with my eyes shut. I am confident that I am *the* hands-down expert at playing that tune – no one else comes close.

passes to say hello because he "always knew you could do it, bro!" and then get a selfie with you and the band...

Won't that feel good?

It's just a matter of time if only you believe it. It's just a matter of when.

But it's going to take work. *Hard* work. Determination. Not giving up.

Your dream may be different. I wanted to make records and tour the world. That was the exact thing that entered my brain at 15 years old, and I wanted nothing else. Not college, not a practical job, not getting wasted at parties on weekends (unless I was at Miles' house making kids listen to The Damned). I had no backup plan. I'd rather sit at home and practice. Leave me alone with my records and my bass, and I'm good. That filled me up and made me happy.

It's nice to know that I can look back and realize that with my bandmates, together, we sold over 10 million records, and we toured the world and played thousands of gigs everywhere we could. I boarded airplanes and left for years on the road to play for people who loved our music. It was satisfying and fun and filled me with the confidence to achieve other dreams – like write this book.

What is your goal?

If you believe that you can do it – whatever your dream may be – then doubt and insecurity will subside eventually, and you will be filled with the opposite – confidence. Which will then breed *opportunity*.

27

Don't let the naysayers realign you. Don't let them guide you. They don't want you to go on that path that will bring you happiness. They see your confidence and envy it. Keep your eyes on the goal and know that it will get difficult before you can have success. It's not easy. Just remember Brenda's words. You are talented, original, and have something important to say. Don't let distractions waver you from this fact and your goal.

28. SHARE YOURSELF

There used to be a barrier to sharing your music. It was hard, expensive, and time consuming to produce. Today sharing your music is easy.

You've got YouTube, Instagram, TikTok, Facebook, Snapchat and more. Nearly everybody has a smartphone, and they all have great cameras. You have a portable video and audio studio warming up your right front pocket. The downside to how easy it is to share content is that you also have the entire planet as your competition. Everyone else is doing the same thing.

But don't be discouraged! There will always be barriers. They just change their spots. It used to be technology and money, now it's people and content. What you need to do is throw your fear and shame and doubt in the trash can and do a spread-eagle dive into the heart of it all. Go for it. Remember your options...

You're going to do one of two things:

1. Let fear stop you
2. Bravely share what you're making and win

The choice is up to you.

The reason you will **WIN** is because if you do unconditionally share what you're doing, you will find people who appreciate you, and they'll be inspired. They will radiate good mojo and vibes back at you, and you will feel good, too, because human beings like to share. I don't know if you believe me or not, but it's true. It's the reason you're reading this right now. That feeling you have inside. You know you can do more. You *want* to do more.

28

Just start with one simple post. Post yourself practicing the bass. Post yourself *playing* something, or post how it makes you feel. If you do this, I guarantee that you have begun building your audience. Your community. Even if you only have 12 followers and 6 likes. It's worth it. If you reach just one person, then it's worth it.

Not everybody will like your posts. I'm not going to lie to you. The naysayers may surprise you. Maybe it's your uncle from Pensacola, or your second-best friend, an old roommate who will be secretly jealous that you're trying something different. Not to mention all of the internet trolls who have nothing better to do. But you will find *your* people. The ones who give you good energy back. Focus on them and be careful of ones who leave you drained.

Share what you are up to. **DON'T WORRY ABOUT HOW THE POST IS RECEIVED**. This is **VITAL**. Just do it without needing anything in return. It will be good for you.

29. DIY FIRST SONGS

You may be thinking... Wait... huh? First songs? This is supposed to be about Basics. Writing seems advanced.

I want to challenge you. To think differently. I want you to open your mind to the possibility that anything is possible. Even writing a song. Maybe we'll start with something more basic. Let's call it a riff. I want you to believe that you can write a cool riff... right now. Even if you got your bass a week ago. Heck, yesterday. I want you to believe you can make something good, something worthy, right now. I know you can. But you must believe it first.

Some writing is advanced. I'll give you that. But not all. Think about some of the greatest riffs of all time. They're simple: "Seven Nation Army" is not a complicated riff. You could have written that. "Whole Lotta Love" is just a blues riff. "My Girl" is simple. "Fly" from my band is beyond simple. It's just two notes. I did add the high F# when I played the D, which made it sound fatter, and more interesting... but who's noticing that? Let me be clear – I'm not saying that coming up with one of those riffs will make you write a hit like The Temptations, The White Stripes, Led Zeppelin, or even Sugar Ray. You need other talented and willing band members to execute the rest. What I am saying is those songs all had to start somewhere. And if you offer up a cool little riff, who knows where you and your friends might take it?

It's good to tap into that childlike excitement, that passion, that fun we all have for music, and remember how it feels. When we get older, we lose touch with the impossible. We start to consider things that we can't do. *Shouldn't* do. You might even have some fear or doubt about playing bass. The only thing that matters is that you are excited to be here, and you will make good things happen.

After a string of international
smash hits, Karges Jr ponders his
future if he can't deliver another
chart-topping record for the label.

THINK OF IT AS A TOY

Before you crush yourself with practice, before you dig into the hours of solitude, plodding through scales, I want you to be free on it, even with little to zero technique or skill. You CAN make sounds on it, and cool sounds at that in these early stages of learning. Nowhere is it written that you have to be good, or skilled, to start making things up. You're free to do that now.

In fact, as we're starting out, I want you to think of your bass guitar as a toy. I don't want you to think of it as a complicated contraption. It's just a toy, you're *supposed* to play with it. It's called *playing* bass. So make sounds. Experiment. Approach it with an open mind. Why not? Maybe try to use a slide on the strings. Why not? If you don't have a slide, just grab anything metal and slide it on the strings by the pickups, holding down notes on the fretboard with your other hand. Make some crazy sounds. See what happens. If you wanted to cut to the chase and get to writing, then here's how you do it. The two-step formula for writing a great riff or song:

1. FIND SOMETHING COOL
2. REPEAT IT

That's it. That's how great songs are written. Listen to classic riffs - that's what they're doing. They've found something cool that they like (a riff or a progression or a motif) and they repeat it. Yes, there are harder riffs to write, but this is a book about basics!

I want to tell you a story about how I wrote my first song on bass. The truth is, I don't remember how long it was before I owned the bass before I wrote it. It feels like it was a week. That's what I like to say. But it was probably a month or so because YOU DO need to learn how to make sounds come from it. No matter how excited you are, it takes some time in the beginning to get your fingers up to speed. I'm not trying to sugar coat that. Your fingers will hurt because bass strings are big and gnarly to play. Guitarists have it easier. That's why guitarists are always so skinny and weak. Bassists' arms and fingers are stronger. Facts.

My first bass was a crappy, used, little blue thing that was not special. But it was special to *me*. It was used and all dinged up, but I loved it. I started making sounds on it immediately. I couldn't play well. Luckily, I was too ignorant to care or understand. I just loved that I could make sounds on it.

I played it through a Peavy guitar amp with a reverb channel because that's all I had. I cranked the reverb because I thought it sounded cool. I loved the sound of it. Nobody told me **you're not supposed to play bass with reverb**. I'm glad no one ever told me. I might have stopped exploring sounds and feeling free to do so.

Soon after I got it, I wrote my first song. It's just a little progression of ringing notes, but I liked it. I'll never forget it. I played the high F note (3rd fret 2nd string) along with the open G string (1st string open) and then I just moved the F down every so often, by half steps, until I was playing the open D and open G together. And then it would loop back and start again. And that was it. It had some decent melodic intentions to it, but I'm not even sure it was a song. It was just a little thing, a jam, but I was too ignorant to understand this, plus I'd only been playing bass for a few weeks. I'm not trying to be cool and say it wasn't good. I wish I was like Jeff Buckley and all my undiscovered early demos and rehearsal tapes had an underlying taste of genius, but alas, it's not true. They were pretty horrible. But it didn't matter. I was happy, and that was all that mattered. Even though I couldn't sing or hit notes well with my voice, my best asset was that I didn't care.

I'm glad my friends in that first band never put a hand on me and said, *"Hey Murph, you have a lot of ideas, and it seems like you want to sing, but you're really flat and you can't hit the notes right, so you should give it up and just play bass."* They wouldn't have been wrong. But the key is that they never said it, so I kept going. Thanks Chris and Eric, for never telling me I sucked.

I wish I could sit in a room with you, turn up the amps, crank some reverb, and just jam with you. You could even sing out of key, and I wouldn't say a damn thing. Why would I? I want you to let go of your perception of what being good is, being 'right' (f**k that) and explore your bass in a place where no one judges you. I don't care where it is. Find it. Even if it's with headphones on in your kitchen at midnight. Just find it.

Now get back to your bass. Explore. Have a great time.

ACTION STEPS

1. Try to write your first riff. Just remember what I said about finding something cool then repeating it. Go for it!

2. If nothing is coming to you, no matter how simple you try to keep it, remember my advice in chapter 16 and go back and listen to some music to inspire you. Nothing still, then go for a car ride and keep listening to music. Something will come. Just give it time.

30. ROCKING OUT LIVE

I started this book talking about playing in front of 55,000 people, and I want to end this book by talking about the thrill of playing live.

That's the ultimate test of how well you've learned to play the bass. Because there's nothing on earth like a live response at a show. It's so intense and nerve wracking, and you get your answer very quickly. They don't have to clap and applaud if they don't want to. If you suck. If you are ill-prepared. They can sit there, after all your hard work to perform a song, and you'll hear crickets. The feedback is instant, and sometimes, brutal. On the other hand, if the crowd bursts into applause, if they cheer, if they chant your name, if their faces light up at what you've offered, then there is no greater feeling.

Playing my bass in front of a crowd was the ultimate dream when I was a kid. Since we had no internet, Google, YouTube, or MTV, **we had no way to preview what was coming in terms of live concerts**. No way to preview the power of how hard those bands would hit when they burst onto the stage and tore into the first song. Rock 'n' roll concerts from the mid-to-late '70s left a huge impression because it was a totally new experience.

You couldn't prepare for it. It would be like skydiving out of an airplane if you had to keep your eyes closed until the moment you jumped. You just didn't know what it would feel like until you felt it. And when you felt it – when that band took the stage and burst into the first song on the loudspeakers – BAM! – it was a feeling that would never leave you.

YouTube has introduced a new way for artists to be discovered. I think it's great. It's fantastic that you can be discovered halfway around the world just by uploading a video you shot in your bedroom on your iPhone. In your pajamas. It's amazing. More young artists are getting discovered on YouTube than ever, and that number will only grow. Other social media channels are coming up every season – Instagram, Snapchat, Tik Tok, etc.

As great as those new avenues are, you still need to play in front of humans. You still need people in front of you. Even if it's in your high school talent show, or your local coffee shop, or open mic night at a club. Anywhere. Take what you've learned here and get in front of people. Take a shot at performing.

Prepare, work hard, and put it all together to play for a live audience. I promise you it won't suck. In fact, it may change your life.

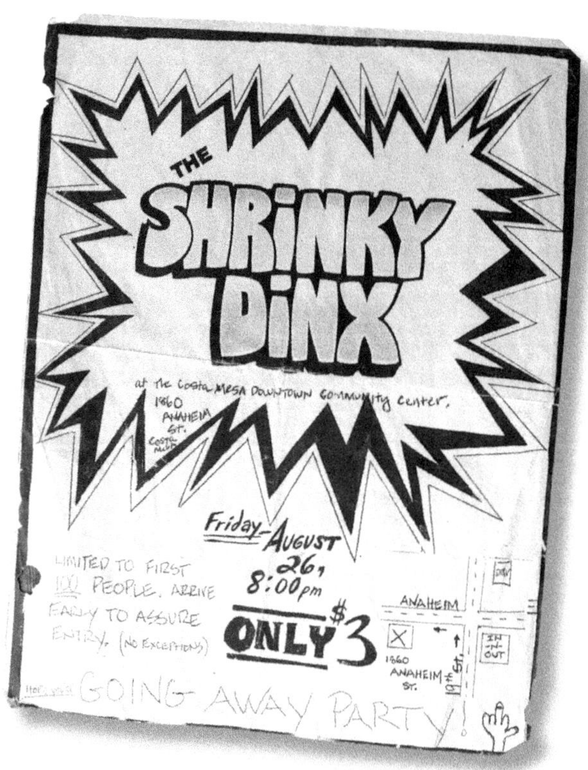

MY FIRST BAND 'THE SHRINKY DINX' TAKE THE COMMUNITY CENTER BY STORM.

Dave Grohl when he is rocking 20,000 people *or* Dave Grohl when he is being tickled – same face.

GRATITUDE

Thank you for buying this book and going on a journey with me to learn how to play bass and understand modern music a little better. I know how long it took to write it, and I also understand your commitment to going through every chapter, taking it all in, and attempting to put it to work.

The reason why I'm grateful to you for reading this book is because going through all these chapters, all the way to the **END**, I know you have the commitment it will take to follow your dreams and become the bass player and musician you want to be. In doing that, you've made me a small part of your journey, and I'm grateful to be connected to you. Because that's what it's about. The goal is to fulfill our own, unique potential. Not to be a carbon copy of someone else. We need our heroes; they help us imagine a different life. They help illuminate a path that has yet to be walked. But make no mistake. The goal is to bring *your unique talent and vision to life*. To be the best version of **YOU**.

Out of the entire book, my greatest joy would be that I helped you learn to enjoy the bass a little more. To realize what a fun, mysterious, and cool instrument it can be. To learn to explore more, to be free from judgement and create sounds on it just because you can, and to do that in creative ways that make no sense. To also learn that it's okay to take your time, be patient, and feel happy about one tiny little success, no matter how small it seems. The gift of music is a deep and mysterious thing, and so why put it in a box?

If you did enjoy this book, and you wanted to share your experience with me, there are a few ways to reach me. You can reach me through the contact form at murphykarges.com, DM on Instagram (my handle is murphykarges), or leave a comment on my latest YouTube video. I read them all. I want to hear about your first DIY riff or about how your jam session went. I will write you back. Or send me a video link to my IG or YouTube channel. I won't judge you. I know what it's like. I know **EXACTLY** what it's like.

Keep playing music, keep playing bass, and I'll see you soon.

ABOUT THE AUTHOR

Murphy Karges is the founding bassist and co-songwriter for the multi-platinum band Sugar Ray. He has five BMI Pop Awards and a Blockbuster Award for Favorite Modern Rock Group that got damaged in a move. Murphy is a self-taught musician who combines his love of playing and his perspectives on music to help others improve. He lives in Newport Beach, California, and online at MurphyKarges.com.

ACKNOWLEDGMENTS

This book is about playing bass and understanding music. Stopping short of thanking my jazz band teacher in high school who told me I'd never amount to anything, (he didn't, he just ignored me) I'd like to thank the people who inspired, encouraged, or assisted me in any way, small or large, to complete this book.

I would like to thank my mom and dad for having a fantastic music collection, and for playing records constantly when Terry, Stacy and I were little kids running around the house. I don't know of any parents who played records more often. All that music is still stuck inside my head. To anyone who wonders why I constantly tap my fingers or float off to another place in my mind, you know who to blame.

Thank you to my big brother Terry for turning me onto good music when I was a teenager, and to Stacy, for always being my biggest fan.

Thanks to Julie, my beautiful wife, who gave me time and space (a LOT of time and space) to create this book. It took two years to write, edit, re-write, re-edit, and so on. Thank you for your patience and for your belief in me.

Thanks to my boys, Matthew Jr., Andrew, and John, for being exactly who you are, every day.

Thank you to my editors, Matt Price and Erica Karlin, for offering your talent and time, and not getting mad at how many times (impossible to count) I started a sentence with "So." Erica, (the goddess of grammar), your advice and suggestions were what I needed to hear, plus you made the intro 10x better. Matt, I appreciate your wit and skill for turning a pile of words into a coherent flow and for never letting me forget how much fun playing music should be.

Thank you to a true all-star of the project, Paul Palmer-Edwards, who forged my 35,000 words, scribblings, and photos into a hand-drawn and custom-created book in a simple and easy-to-digest way without ever being boring or repetitive. Thank you for putting in the hours you did.

Thank you to Jack Grisham. You challenged me with great questions and said something positive about my writing – years ago. You might not even remember, but it stuck with me. Thanks to Stan Frazier, who endured my constant phone calls and questions about what bands and songs I should include in the book.

Thank you to everyone who has subscribed to my YouTube channel. I love the community we have created, I appreciate your comments, ideas, and opinions, and I look forward to the new friendships and discussions this book will create.

Thanks to all the musicians I have ever jammed with, or bands I have been in, past and present. It is always a learning experience. Except for that one heavy metal guy from San Clemente. I have no idea what that was.

I probably learned the most about being a musician during my 23 years in Sugar Ray, writing, recording, and playing alongside Craig, Mark, Rodney, and Stan. We had some amazing times together and I am forever grateful for that.

I would also like to thank: Annie Wilson-Karges, the Writer's Den at Chateau Mimi, Burke Thomas, "Iron" Mike Savoia, Frank Micelotta, Spencer Askin, Melissa Elhardt, Brenda Ueland, my 13" Macbook Pro, and maybe most especially to all the fans who have come out to countless shows over the years to hear my bandmates and me do our damndest to create music that you often seem to enjoy as much as we do. Eternally grateful.

CONTINUE LEARNING

WWW.MURPHYKARGES.COM

YouTube.com/@MurphyKargesBass

Instagram.com/MurphyKarges

Facebook.com/MurphyKargesBass